I direct this series to those moving in the wind of the Aquarian cycle. To those who would move into the new dispensation yet know not the way to go I say, there is a Path. Step by step it has been carved by the initiates of the sacred fire. Over thousands of years the barefooted devotees have worn a trail over the rocks.

The way is known of us. It can also be known by you. In support of Saint Germain, Master of the Aquarian Age, exponent of the flame of freedom to mankind, I place the jewel of my crown upon the altar of the Great White Brotherhood, that those who have lost the way may find it again.

The path to our abode is steep. The way is fraught with unknown dangers, yet the peaks of pride are more jagged than the uncharted heights. I come to clear the way for the chelas of God's will—those who would become chelas of the ascended masters.

Whether Christian or Jew, Moslem or Zen Buddhist, or none of these, know, O seeker after higher reality, that the path of initiation can be trod wherever you are. But *you* must take the first step. My responsibility is to guide and guard: yours is to follow.

With the full faculties of mind and heart and soul, you chart the course of your life.

El Morya

The Chela and the Path

Keys to Soul Mastery in the Aquarian Age

Ascended Master
El Morya

Dictated to the Messenger
Elizabeth Clare Prophet

SUMMIT UNIVERSITY ◐ PRESS®

THE CHELA AND THE PATH:
Keys to Soul Mastery in the Aquarian Age
by El Morya. Dictated to Elizabeth Clare Prophet.
Copyright © 1975, 1976 Summit University Press. All rights reserved.

Library of Congress Catalog Card Number: 76-7634
ISBN: 0-922729-33-6

Cover: Oil painting entitled *The Chela on the Path* by Norman
Thomas Miller

SUMMIT UNIVERSITY ♥ PRESS®
Summit University Press and ♥ are registered trademarks.

This book is set in Baskerville.
Printed in the United States of America

The paper used in this publication meets the requirements of the
American National Standards Institute Z39.48-1992 (Permanence
of Paper).

CONTENTS

I dedicate these letters to all who share the dream of freedom and good will among men and nations— to all who know that the only means to achieve that goal is the path of initiation. May the dream of Camelot come true because real knights and ladies of the flame live today who by love, sacrifice, and self-discipline will make that dream come true.

The Ascended Master El Morya

Beloved Chelas Who Would Be on the Path with Morya—

This book contains keys we all need to know in order to meet the challenge of life in today's world. That challenge is to understand and to be who and what we are—right in the midst of the turbulent uncertainties, the disintegration of self-awareness, and the monolith of mechanization that mark this civilization. Our very life, even the integration of consciousness itself, is at stake in the challenge of just living from day to day.

Just when all of the manipulations of a synthetic society seem to be massaging our senses into subtle and strange compartments of unreality, the Ascended Master El Morya comes with the Christ and the Buddha to point the way out of the dilemma posed by the world's delusions—the dichotomy of the self deceived by the self and the duality to which we have conditioned ourselves by our sense of sin and struggle and shame.

Who is the Ascended Master El Morya? Indeed, who are we? El Morya's credibility lies in the fact that he has attained to the enlightenment of the Buddha and the ascension of the Christ. What's more, he says that if we follow the same teachings of the gurus which he has followed, we too can attain. And then this will be *our* credibility.

El Morya is an ascended master. Western saint turned Eastern adept, he takes on chelas, or students, of the masters of both East and West and initiates them in the rigors of the ascension. The ascension: path of Jesus, Mary, Saint Germain, of Gautama and Maitreya and the patriarchs and prophets of Israel. The ascension: goal of soul-liberation through reunion with that which was, is, and ever will be—the I AM THAT I AM.

El Morya has raised consciousness, soul, mind, and body

from planes of mortality to spheres of immortality. El Morya is one with every son and daughter of God and the great hosts of the Lord who have done the same—accelerated the atom of the nonpermanent self to become the Permanent Self. Together with devotees in embodiment, these emissaries of God comprise the Great White Brotherhood.*

The Great White Brotherhood is that confraternity of saints and sages of East and West who have risen from every walk of life, religion, race, and nation to minister to the souls of humanity anywhere and everywhere there is a need. El Morya's service to the Brotherhood is carried out in his presiding role as Chief of the Darjeeling Council. Meeting in his Darjeeling retreat, the Temple of Good Will, the council is a 'round table' of ascended masters and their unascended chelas who study and recommend solutions to the world's political and economic problems and sponsor and train students and statesmen who serve humanity under the ray of God's will, the first ray, of which El Morya is the chohan (lord or authority).

Once an unascended chela, now the ascended guru, the master comes to clear the way for the chelas of God's will, and he says, "Let the chips fall where they may!" Morya, the beloved, has entered the temple of the will of God within his own being, there to find the Christ and the Buddha of his own soul. And out of his soul's communion with the Law of the One, he has defined the Goal and mapped out the most direct, hence the most rugged, approach to the summit of being. For those who value footprints in the sands of time and space—the footprints of a living ascended master—El Morya is the one. His fearsome look, his fearlessness, the lightning and the thunder of his presence, these are the resolute expressions of his absolute devotion to the chela on the Path.

Morya is a guru of gurus and so loved by his chelas because he is direct, uncircumscribed, and entirely uninhibited. Morya is the original and only Morya. His motto: Expect the unexpected. His chastisements, filled with his love for the will of

---

*"White" does not refer to race but to the aura of white light that surrounds them.

God for each evolving soul, never leave his chelas hopeless or the hapless victims of their karma, but always in the joyous challenge to come up higher. Morya says: "Leave the rags of your lesser self for the robes of your Real Self—thou who art forevermore a priest after the Order of Melchizedek!"

For those who would realize their true identity in Christ and in Buddha, El Morya—the incomparable, the unconquerable—is the most valuable guide on the Path. He prepares the chela to meet his very own God Presence and to contact the Real Self, the individual Christ, the only component of being through which his soul can survive his experiences in time and space. El Morya, "a chela of the one Guru," drills his chelas for entrance into the etheric retreats of the Great White Brotherhood and for their tutelage under the great master Saint Germain, hierarch of the Aquarian age, or in the classes of Serapis Bey, hierarch of the Ascension Temple at Luxor, Egypt.

El Morya, the great devotee of the will of God, prepares his chelas for every eventuality they will encounter along the spectrums of expanding cosmic consciousness. Once you have been through El Morya's school of testing and more testing in the experiences of day-to-day life on earth and then the inner retreat experience—to which he bids all readers of this work—you know that you have been duly trained for the Path. You also know that any failure is your own. For Morya takes on only the stalwart—those for whom the trek upward is worth the inconvenience.

By the direct and penetrating gaze of his eye—that is at once upon the eye of God and the eye of the chela—El Morya guards the devotees of universal good will from the pitfalls of self-indulgence and from the "way which seemeth right"—as the proverb says, "but the end thereof are the ways of death." If you will submit your will to the will of God, Morya will stand by you, your advocate before the Father, until you are counted with the overcomers who have gone before through the open door of the Christ and the Buddha into octaves of light and realms of radiant reality. Here your soul reunited with your own

I AM Presence will dwell forevermore in the sanctuary of the Most High—a son, a daughter of God, an ascended master.

The genius of *The Chela and the Path* lies in the vast perspective of the author as well as in his absolute integrity, evidenced not only by the historical facts of his soul's illustrious incarnations on earth (recounted in the biographical sketch at the back of the book), but also by his ongoing relationship with his chelas that spans the centuries. One and all they will tell you of his very powerful presence, personally directing their chelaship, cutting each facet of the diamond of self-awareness according to the inner blueprint that is the will of God for every soul.

Once you have won the guru's heart, and there is only one way—by the courage to "love one another as I have loved you" and to be the self-disciplined devotee of God's will—Morya will be to you the truest friend you have ever known. As the guru he will put himself on the line for you—your sponsor before the Lords of Karma. Paul said, "Ye are bought with a price." Only the guru knows what price he must pay for his chela's opportunity to be chela. Morya, unmoved by the betrayers of his trust, stands ready to pay the price for the chela who wills to be the will of God.

El Morya lived as the brilliant mathematician and astrologer, Melchior, the wise man who visited the infant Messiah at his birth. As King Arthur, he governed the vast territory of Britain and instituted the council of the Round Table. As Thomas Becket, first as Lord Chancellor and then as Archbishop of Canterbury under Henry II, he gave his life to preserve the Church from royal aggression. Later as Thomas More, again in the role of Lord Chancellor of England, he died a martyr in defense of religious principle. As Akbar the Great, Mogul emperor of India, he established order through enlightenment in a period of great turbulence and strife. Then as the poet Thomas Moore, he became loved and honored as the national lyricist of Ireland. He ascended at the conclusion of the nineteenth century following his efforts with the Masters K.H., D.K., the Count Saint Germain, and H. P. Blavatsky in founding the Theosophical Society.

In 1958 El Morya founded The Summit Lighthouse through his beloved chela, the Messenger Mark L. Prophet, for the purpose of publishing the teachings of the ascended masters. After my training under Mark and Morya, Saint Germain anointed me messenger in order that Mark and I, as twin flames, might set forth the sacred scriptures for the Aquarian age. Not a channel, not a spiritualistic medium, the messenger of the Great White Brotherhood stands at the level of the Real Self, transferring the light of hierarchy in order that the student might make contact with his own Real Self, the inner Guru, through the Word and the Presence of the ascended masters.

Mark took his leave of this octave, as he had told me he would, and made his ascension in February of 1973. Today the Ascended Master Lanello, he is recognized by his students around the world as he manifests himself to them, the ever-present Guru, while I, vested by Saint Germain with the office of Mother of the Flame, continue by God's grace to instruct and initiate students of the ascended masters at Summit University. With sweet affection for the Flame, devotees call me Mother in honor of the one I adore. And so here at our Camelot come again, God is working his work through us in conducting conferences and retreats, in recording the teachings, and in directing the multifaceted activities of Church Universal and Triumphant, including a full year-round program for toddlers through sixth grade at Montessori International, a private school using innovative educational techniques. May you also find your place, come again, at one of our quarterly retreats held here in El Morya's Community of the Holy Spirit.

The Chela and the Path contains the teachings of the Ascended Master El Morya which he dictated to me at my retreat in Santa Barbara. In it, he presents a step-by-step analysis of the Greater Self and the lesser self, drawing the threads of reality and truth handed down from the Ancient of Days.

Within the spectrum of the religious and philosophical traditions of East and West, a master of both psychology (the study
of the soul) and science, he presents the law of life taught by
the ascended masters for thousands of years in the retreats of
the Great White Brotherhood. Thus the beloved Master M., as
he has been called for more than a century by students of
Theosophy, presents ultimate answers to the ultimate questions
of life itself: Who am I and where am I going?

Originally published as a series of letters to his students
throughout the world, El Morya's message is intensely personal.
Written somewhat in the tradition of the Zen masters of the
East, even with a touch of the gruff, lovable Bodhidharma, it
has a style all of its own which challenges the ordinary modes
of the mind and compels an extraordinary movement of one's
mentality toward the conquest of the *mount of Mind*. The student is encouraged to follow closely the implications of every
word the Master has dictated—as well as those he has not. In
order to reap full benefit from the master's teaching, one must
be prepared to disengage oneself from the sophistry of the
intellect and "learn to experience life with the faculties of the
soul."

It is the purpose of this book to liberate your soul for the
grand adventure of integration with the Cosmos through the
path of initiation under the ascended masters of the Great
White Brotherhood. May it serve this purpose in your life.
Vondir!

I remain his adoring chela,

Mother

CHAPTER 1

Chelas of the Will of God:

The tall pines of Darjeeling move against the morning light. A day is born. It is a day of opportunity. Just as knowledge that is unused is lost, so knowledge without love is brittle. The mists in the foothills are for the watering of life. And the love of the Holy Spirit nourishes the soul in time of travail.

The path to our abode is steep. The way is fraught with unknown dangers, yet the peaks of pride are more jagged than the uncharted heights. I come to clear the way for the chelas of God's will—those who would become chelas of the ascended masters.

Let it be made clear at the beginning that all who read the words of the ascended masters and all who hear our word are not necessarily counted as chelas of our will. Let it be quite clear that there are requirements. As the chips of wood fly when the pines in the forest are cleared, so the winds of Darjeeling blow. Let the unworthy chela be cleared from our path. We clear for a noble purpose—the ennoblement of a cause and a race. Hierarchy has also said, "Let the chips fall where they may!"

The strong gaze of the true master is upon the stalwart.

The weak-willed, unable to look upon their own image, can scarcely receive our eye. I write for those who have a will to change; for transmutation is the requirement of the hour. I direct this series to those moving in the wind of the Aquarian cycle. To those who would move into the new dispensation yet know not the way to go I say, there is a path. Step by step it has been carved by the initiates of the sacred fire. Over thousands of years the barefooted devotees have worn a trail over the rocks.

The way is known of us. It can also be known by you. In support of Saint Germain, Master of the Aquarian Age, exponent of the flame of freedom to mankind, I place the jewel of my crown upon the altar of the Great White Brotherhood, that those who have lost the way may find it again.

As it is written in scripture, "There is a way that seemeth right unto a man, but the end thereof are the ways of death."[1] The way that seemeth right is the way of reason—and that not of the eternal Logos, but of the consciousness that is bound to the laws of mortality. Hence its ways are the ways of the death of the Christ consciousness.

I am come to bring life in the tradition of the Master of Galilee. He came that all might have life, and that more abundantly.[2] His way is the way of grace. His grace is oil for the gears of the law and for the meshing of the teeth of the deeds of righteousness. I would free those who would be freed.

Until men recognize the darkness, they do not reach for the light. Thus the grossness of materialism and of a mechanistic civilization continues unchallenged. To challenge, men must have a sword; and the sword is the sacred Word of truth to this age.

The Darjeeling Council is a unit of hierarchy. I am its chief. Numbered among those who deliberate in our chambers are Saint Germain, Mary the Mother, Jesus the Christ, the Master Kuthumi, Chananda, the Great Divine Director, Lord Maitreya, and the Ascended Master Godfre. Assisted by many unascended chelas, we serve the cause of the will of God among humanity, in the governments of the nations, in the economic councils, in the social strata, in the institutions of learning, and above all, in the diamond hearts of the devotees.

Those who see the crumbling of the old order look for the new. The path of chelaship is the way of transition. For those who would arrive at the station of the new cycle, we provide answers and a formula. And there is no turning back. In those in whom selfishness has not marred the vision of the new day, there is the burning desire to be free and to make that freedom available to all.

Such was the purpose of the Darjeeling Council in the founding of The Summit Lighthouse in Washington, D.C., in 1958. With humble beginnings, yet with the torch of our trust passed from God and anchored in the heart of a band of devotees, we built our organization—an outer arm of the Great White Brotherhood, a forum for the will of God, a focus for the purity of its fiery core.

Mark Prophet—and later his twin flame, Elizabeth— was trained by me to be a messenger for that hierarchy of adepts composed of all who have graduated from earth's schoolroom with honor. These are they who have mastered the laws of their own karma and by the pursuit of the Buddhic light have been thrust from the wheel of rebirth. These are the ascended ones whose souls have been lifted into the glory of the life universal and triumphant. By their striving on the way, by their excellence in self-discipline, and by the grace of Christ, they are the overcomers.[3] Having not been found wanting in any thing, they have entered into eternal communion with the fount of reality through the ritual of the ascension.

To ascend into the plane of reality as they have done, you must garner within your soul the thrust of power, wisdom, and love. To transcend planes of consciousness, to make the giant leap into the arms of God—this requires thrust. Therefore from the wellspring of life, out of the fount of living flame which Almighty God has anchored within your heart, draw forth the thrust of faith, hope, and charity.

Whether Christian or Jew, Moslem or Zen Buddhist, or none of these, know, O seeker after higher reality, that the path of initiation can be trod wherever you are. But *you* must take the first step. My responsibility is to guide and guard: yours is to follow.

With the full faculties of mind and heart and soul, you chart the course of your life. If you desire, the grid of hierarchy and of initiation through hierarchy can be superimposed upon your chart. If you have not the desire for initiation, if there be no longing to replace the old man with the new,[4] if there be no desiring for freedom, then you cannot magnetize the molecules of our momentum on the path, nor will you magnetize the mind of the Great Initiator who provides not only the testing, but the wherewithal to pass the tests.

Hierarchy comes forth to reveal truth to the age. We gather together the atoms of self-determination. The new year is the open door for initiation. Our call is to the many who have come of age, who are ready to be received by their own Christ-identity. For the dispensation has gone forth from the Lords of Karma that a million souls presently evolving on this planet—a certain million whose evolutionary time has come—might be given a more than ordinary assistance on the path of life. These will feel the emanations of our word. These will know the presence of the ascended masters. Though yet unseen, that presence will be clearly marked by divine direction and by inspiration leading to solutions to current world problems.

To chelas throughout the world I dictate this series through our messenger, Elizabeth Clare Prophet, called by Saint Germain to hold the office of Mother of the Flame. Let all who are moved by the flame of their own consciousness to pursue the high road of inner reality elect to follow the path of the elect of God. These are they who throughout the ages, in every walk of life, both within and without the Church, have chosen the bands of his will. These have banded together to define the laws of science, mathematics, and the geometry of the soul; these have pursued culture, education, the arts and music out of the desiring to merge with the laws of cosmos that are the will of every man's being.

Let all who perceive the need to nourish the flame of consciousness prepare to work with the Mother of the Flame and the Darjeeling masters for the enlightenment of the race through the discipline of the self.

I AM a mentor of the Spirit,

El Morya

CHAPTER 2

Chelas of East and West:

The thought form for the year 1975 released by the Lord of the World, Gautama Buddha, on New Year's Eve is a lodestone of the mind of God—"a multifaceted jewel focusing the flame of the mind of God, a gem that is not of this world; nor does it bear resemblance to the crystals of this plane. In the center of the jewel is that flame of the mind of God. . . . This jewel is anchored in the etheric plane of the planet at the retreat at Shamballa. And the fire of God's mind focused therein will be for the quickening of the consciousness of mankind in the way of truth and the restoration of balance, of vision infusing the mind with that love that enables life to impart a gnosis of the Logos."[1]

The seven holy Kumaras, lords of flame from Venus, are the sponsors of mankind's mental development. Over the thousands of years of earth's history, they have come forward at certain auspicious moments to raise the energies of consciousness, to accelerate the action of the Christ mind, to polarize mankind's energies in the upper chakras. Thus the anchoring (in all who will make the call) of the jewel replica of the mind of God at the etheric level between the pineal and the pituitary glands is for the activation of the flame of the Logos to further enhance the initiations of a planet and a people on the path of hierarchy.

Just as there are many would-be chelas in the world, so there are many who *could* be chelas who know nothing of the path or of chelaship. There are still others who, for lack of outer contact with our representatives, walk the earth as chelas yet know not that they are as chelas nor that they have our guidance on the path. What, then, is chelaship?

Chela is a term meaning student or disciple of a religious teacher. It is derived from the Hindi *celā,* which is taken from the Sanskrit *ceta,* meaning slave. In the Eastern tradition of chelaship, recognized for thousands of years as the way of self-mastery and enlightenment, one desiring to have the mysteries of universal law imparted to him applies to the teacher, known as the guru, considered to be a master (through the ages the real gurus have included both ascended and unascended masters) to serve that teacher until he is found worthy to receive the keys to his own inner reality.

The great yogi Milarepa endured many hardships on the path, including the unlearning of the false teachings of the dark ones who imparted to him a knowledge of the manipulation of energy. Thus he had to overcome the practice of black magic and to balance the karma of his misdeeds whereby he had wreaked vengeance upon his neighbors who had deprived him of his patrimony, first causing the death of many and then a hailstorm which destroyed their fields of barley ripe for the harvest. When he finally earned the right to be the chela of a true master, his pride had been broken and in humility he walked the way of attainment.

In the Eastern tradition, the chela is the slave of his

master for a good reason—not for the loss of his true identity, but for the replacement of the pseudoimage with the
Real Image of selfhood. The chela, by submission, day by day
is weaving into consciousness the threads of the garment of
his master. The master's garment (as the much sought-after
robe of the Christ) is synonymous with the master's consciousness.

In return for illumined obedience and self-sacrificing
love, the chela receives increments of the master's attainment—of the master's own realization of his Real Self.
Through the acceptance of the word of the master as invio-
late, the chela has imparted to him the Christ consciousness
of his master, which in turn is the means whereby the base
elements of the chela's subconscious and the momentums
of his untransmuted karma are melted by the fervent heat
of the sacred fire which comprises the master's consciousness. Thus by freely and willingly setting aside the momentums of his human consciousness, the chela discovers that
these are soon replaced by his teacher's mastery, which,
when he makes it his own, serves as the magnet to magnetize his own higher consciousness and attainment.

Those who have observed this process have remarked in
their ignorance that the chelas of the ascended master or of
the unascended masters are somehow hypnotized, or duped,
or perhaps even controlled like robots. They have not understood the path of surrender. They have not perceived the
path as the shortcut to that enlightenment and that freedom
which they still seek in the world, knowing not that the
world can never impart to them the freedom and the enlightenment of their soul's desiring.

Thus one man's bondage is another man's freedom; one
man's freedom is another man's bondage. In truth all

mankind are prisoners of their own karma, and all mankind are liberated through their own karma. This means that the causes which mankind have set in motion in previous embodiments produce the effects that reverberate in the world of today from the personal to the planetary level. And that which seems to be happenstance or the configurations of astrology all have but one source—past actions coming full circle according to the law of cycles.

The true teacher teaches the chela how to come to grips with his karma—past, present, and future. He shows him how to study the law of causation in his own life and to trace undesirable conditions of the present to the core of past actions and interactions with individuals, family members, and the world at large. Thus the reactions of the past produce the ramifications of the present; and step by step the chela is taught to withdraw from the fabric of consciousness the blackened threads of unwise sowings of the past, that he might reap a more abundant harvest in the karma of the future.

To do this the chela must transcend the former state of consciousness; else he will repeat the same mistakes. To transcend that state, he must break through the paper bag of his own finite awareness—the cul-de-sac of mortal reason in which he has been floundering for centuries of incarnations. Thus when the pupil is ready for the breakthrough, the teacher appears.

The Master Kuthumi once wrote to a would-be chela about "forcing" the master to receive him. For, you see, by cosmic law the ascended masters *must* take on as their chelas those who move and act in conformity with the will of God on the path of self-discipline and self-immolation. When the chela, by unflinching service, shows himself to be indeed a slave of the diamond-shining mind of God, refusing to bow down to other idols of lesser selfhood, he finds himself standing face to face with either an ascended or unascended master of the Great White Brotherhood or one of our embodied representatives who will provide him with certain teachings and practical steps to attain the goal of reunion whereby the outer consciousness meshes with the inner consciousness and the soul expresses the full potential of its innate Godhood.

As is often the case, the ascended masters remain behind the veil, which means simply that because of a lack of surrender or a lack of development in the chela, they retain a certain anonymity and prefer to remain elusive to the outer consciousness, almost playing hide-and-seek with the chela. And this is a means of keeping the chela in hot pursuit of the guru; for it is the striving—the intense striving—for oneness that is the mark of the overcomer.

Throughout the ages those disciples who have been willing to submit totally in the ritual that is known as the "submission unto love" have made the most rapid strides and sometimes in a single lifetime have balanced enough karma to secure the nirvanic union which we prefer to call the ascension in the light. Such a one was John the Beloved, who through love rose above the twelve and was the only disciple to attain the ascension at the close of the Galilean mission.

As you meditate upon your place upon the path, upon the circumstances of your life—what you are, what you desire to be, where you are and where you desire to be—consider that love is the fulfilling of the law of the path of chelaship. And if you would enter that path as the shortcut to self-awareness, you must be fearless in your acceptance of his word "He who seeks to save his life shall lose it; but he who loses his life for my sake shall find it."[2]

He who spoke these words serves today with the Master Kuthumi in the office of World Teacher. He is a teacher who has thousands of followers—some devotees, some disciples. But in the strictest sense of the word, the chelas of Jesus Christ are few and far between. For a lack of love and for a lack of laying down one's life for one's friends, those who are the would-be chelas of the Christ, those who could be, fall short of the mark of this high calling.

From the temple of God's Will high in the Himalayas there is the sounding of the ancient bell. It is a call to the humble the world around, to the servants of the will of God, and to the avant-garde who would carry civilization forward into a new age. Morya summons chelas of the sacred fire who would become adepts, followers who would become friends of Christ, exponents of the word of living truth, imitators of the master, and finally the heart, head, and hand of our cosmic retinue.

We seek planetary alignment. We seek to overshadow, to become one with, to work through—yea, to pour the essence of our selfhood into hearts uplifted, the chalice of consciousness raised on high. We demand the all of those to whom we would give our all. The question is, Are you ready to exchange your lesser self for our Greater Self?

The path that offers much requires much. As you say in the world, you get what you pay for. The price is high, but then you are purchasing the ultimate reality.

I AM a guru of many chelas and a chela of the one Guru.

CHAPTER 3

Very Important Chapter

Chelas in the Way of Self-Mastery:

What is the mastery of the self? To properly answer this question, we must first define the self. Know, O chela of the light, that you are what you are regardless of what you think you are. The affirmation of the Real Self of every man and woman—the declaration of being and consciousness—is I AM WHO I AM.[1]

From out the white-fire core of the individualization of the God flame, the eternal Presence declares the geometry of self-realization. A God is born. And out of that God, self-awareness, as a ball of identity, is thrust into the planes of Matter. The ball, a microcosm of selfhood flung from far-off worlds, is an extension of the Great Spirit. It is an extension of God-selfhood, of self-awareness in other dimensions.

The ball is a microcosm spun out of the great Macrocosm of all-pervading consciousness that men call God. The ball of self is suspended in that consciousness, tethered to its source by the thread of contact that is called the crystal cord. And so the ball of identity, like a child's toy bouncing from an elastic string tied to a paddle, is free to move in time and space, yet ever subject to the movement of the hand of the Great Law that governs its comings and its goings in finite dimensions.

"O Lord our Lord, how excellent is thy name in all the earth! who hast set thy glory above the heavens. . . .When I consider thy heavens, the work of thy fingers, the moon and the stars, which thou hast ordained, what is man, that thou art mindful of him? and the son of man, that thou visitest him? For thou hast made him a little lower than the angels and hast crowned him with glory and honour. Thou madest him to have dominion over the works of thy hands; thou hast put all things under his feet."[2]

To define the self for those who have not yet realized the self, I must employ terms that you understand in your present twilight awareness, in the hopes that these terms will translate to the outer self certain images of the inner self and thereby provide you with the foundations for an ever-expanding awareness of being.

There is a portion of the self that is immutable. That portion of selfhood that is the permanent atom of being is called the I AM Presence. It is the Monad of Self suspended in the planes of Spirit. It is the Godhead individualized as a living flame, as a point of consciousness, as a sphere of identity. It is God—your God Self.

The goal of life and of self-mastery is to merge with this atom of selfhood that is absolute reality. Thus we have established the purpose for self-mastery. But we have not entirely defined the self; nor have we answered the question of the chela who has asked, "What is the purpose of selfhood and the self?"

In answer to this question, the Lord Buddha has said, "Only when you realize the full potential of your self will you fully understand the purpose of self." Nonetheless, I am permitted to explain that the nature of God as consciousness is realized in the infinite frequencies of both the spiritual and the material cosmos in aspects of God self-awareness infinitely diversified, infinitely unified. Therefore, if you could dial your own consciousness one by one through the infinite stations, or frequencies, of God's consciousness, by and by through billions of light-years of self-transcending selfhood, you would begin to have a perspective of the constant that is God—a constantly self-transcending energy field.

And now, blessed chelas, lest you despair on the path of discovering the self, let us turn aside for a moment from our self-ponderings of the infinite and see what portion of the Infinite One has been realized in the immediate forcefield of that which you call your self. The seed of this self, of course, had to come forth from the great God Self, for there is no other source from whence it could come. Cycling through the spheres of the great Monad of Life, the seed of self-awareness gathers skeins of light—thread by thread, wound and woven, woven and wound about the point of awareness, building an energy field. And the seed becomes a *soul* born out of *S*pirit's *o*wn *u*nion with *l*ife. And the soul is a miniature sun revolving about the central sun of Universal Being.

You see, the energy that is God, that is the white-fire core of consciousness, is in perfect polarity—plus and minus. The sphere of God-being is a whirling atom that is called the Alpha-to-Omega. Out of the whirling of the polarity of the I AM THAT I AM, the seed of the soul is born. And as it moves through the cycles of the Monad, it forms a new polarity with the center. And the electron of selfhood, a new selfhood, is born.

That electron, when thrust forth from the atom of God's being, is the materialization of the God flame. With the bursting-forth of the negative polarity of the first atom of selfhood, Matter and the material cosmos was born—the counterpart of Spirit and the spiritual cosmos. As God multiplied himself over and over again in the I AM Presence (the individualized spark of being), the seeds that became souls —the souls that were thrust from the planes of Spirit—became living souls in the planes of Matter.

Just as the seed gathered skeins of light to form the identity of the soul, so the emergent souls gathered skeins of Matter to form the vehicles of selfhood in time and space —the mind, the memory, the emotions tethered to the physical form. Thus veiled in flesh and blood, the soul was equipped to navigate in time and space. Billions of seeds of selfhood are evolving in the solar systems that span the far reaches of the material cosmos. Alas, souls evolving in the whirl of energy you call your world have not the perspective of their origin in the vast beyond.

This which you call your self, then, is a finite portion of the infinite, a little world of selfhood destined to one day become, through self-realization, the greater world of selfhood. By free will the souls of man and woman may experiment with the laws governing time and space and may elect, as electrons of the central sun, to return to the white-fire core of being through conformity with the mind of God. Know, O chela of the will of God, that the purpose of the path and of chelaship is that you might bring that portion of selfhood that has separated from the center, that has gone forth into the Matter cosmos, into eternal alignment with the permanent atom of being.

Unfortunately, once the separation occurred, the soul's adaptation to the frequencies of Matter resulted, after millions of years of evolution, in a loss of memory of origin, of true being, and of the wholeness of the self. As the memory of selfhood became more and more obscured by the frequencies of Matter, the mind, the emotions, the form, and the form consciousness were found less and less in conformity with the inner lodestone of reality, the I AM Presence. And by and by these sheaths of awareness that surrounded the soul took on an identity of their own—and a pseudoidentity at that.

This pseudoidentity was molded by the awareness of life in Matter which little by little became independent of the soul's inner awareness of the Real Self. And the sheaths of identity produced a self-identification based upon the mirrored images of selfhood reflected from face to face, from life to life, yet never mirroring the face of reality or the life that is God.

"Now we see through a glass, darkly."[3] To address a civilization that is based solely upon the pseudoimage of selfhood which we call the synthetic image—the image that is a manufactured counterfeit of the Real Self—and to say to that civilization, "That which you think you are, you are not: that which you think you are not, you are," we must appeal to the soul and to the soul's distant memory of reality. This we do in the certainty that the souls who are ready will be quickened. "Then shall two be in the field; the one shall be taken, and the other left."[4]

Our purpose in this series of *Pearls of Wisdom,* O chela, is to take you by the hand and lead you gently from the outer awareness of mind, memory, and emotions—feelings, percepts, and recepts registering through the five senses that are tethered to a material existence—to the inner awareness of the soul through the discipline of energies and consciousness. That portion of the self which you have invested in this outer awareness must be withdrawn from the outer and reinvested in the inner.

At that point we begin the development of the consciousness of the soul that is called solar awareness. Newly born to the soul, you must begin to learn to experience life with the faculties of the soul. Like the five physical senses, these senses of the soul, dormant for aeons, are being quickened by cosmic currents and cosmic rays to realign that which you call your self to the point of identity that is in reality your Real Self.

Until we come together again for the contemplation of the finite self against the backdrop of the Infinite Self, won't you consider the query of the Psalmist "What is man, that thou art mindful of him? and the son of man, that thou visitest him?" Consider how being springs from being springs from being and how molecules of selfhood emerge from other molecules of selfhood, which emerge from still other molecules of self-consciousness. For to become the Real Self, you must meditate upon that self, its origin and destiny—its laws, its geometry.

I have given you a series of expanding matrices designed to expand, through your own meditation, the circumference of self-awareness.

CHAPTER 4

_____

Chelas of the White-Fire Core:

For the purpose of unraveling the skeins of a false identity, we diagram selfhood. As I have said, you are what you
are regardless of what you think you are.

You are in reality a living flame. The flame above is
called the I AM Presence. The flame below is the spark of
life anchored in the center of being. It is a threefold flame
of the Real Self, having the attributes in fire of power, wisdom, and love. This threefold flame is the fire of God that
burns in the plane of Matter to sustain the seed identity that
was and is a living soul.

The many layers of awareness that surround the soul—
the energy fields of mind and memory, emotions, feelings,
physical form, form consciousness, percepts and recepts—
have so polarized selfhood through an outer awareness that
this outer awareness has become a synthetic self diametri-
cally opposed to the Real Self. And the soul that was intended to mirror the Spirit has become a mirror for a world
of whirling energies unlike its original reality, hence unreal.
The soul has become a lost identity, lost in time and space.
It must be found again. It must find itself in God.

Thus we behold the plight of the soul lost in the force-fields of a *sub*consciousness—a self-awareness that is below the threshold of God's Self-awareness which declares, "I AM WHO I AM." Because man and woman were given the gift of free will and the gift of life that is the threefold flame, they may consciously choose to affirm the law of the flame and the identity of the flame and to call that flame "my Self." In so doing male and female return to the divine polarity. In so doing male and female return to the seat of authority— the authority of the Real Self to take dominion over the synthetic self. From that point of self-identification, all may proceed to draw the skeins of the evolving soul identity into the central core of being that is the flame called God.

Now there is an aspect of your self that I would acquaint you with. It is that point of consciousness which knows the Self that is God while knowing the self that is the soul in the state of becoming God. It also knows all of the aspects of awareness tethered to the synthetic image. This point of selfhood we call the Christ Self, or the Anointed One. In the diagram of selfhood it is the mediator between that portion of self evolving in the planes of Spirit which we have called the I AM Presence and that portion of self evolving in the planes of Matter which is known as the seed identity or the soul. (See illustration page 142.)

The Christ Self is your true self. It is what you really are as an individual reflecting the individuality of God. It is your real personality that is a part of the personality of God. The Christ Self is your mentor, your personal guru, until the day when, merging with that self, you affirm, "I AM the Christ, I AM the mentor, I AM the guru." The separation from this self, from this reality, is sustained only so long as you, by your free will, choose to sustain the components of the synthet⸱ image.

Now therefore, since you are what you are, let us consider what you are. In the planes of Matter you are a conglomerate of causation—past, present, and future. You are a forcefield—an energy field—a complex atom of selfhood, an organized coil of identity, a center of soul awareness evolving toward God Self-awareness. As a forcefield of causation, you are an accumulation of karma, of energy that is in positive and negative polarity which must be brought into balance with cosmic law and cosmic cycles, that it might transcend the planes of Matter and overcome the limitations of time and space.

You have the gift of consciousness. Consciousness centered in the flame of life anchored in the heart knows itself as God—as limitless potential, as a being that is infinite though tethered to a matrix that is finite. The flame that you are is the flowing stream of consciousness that ever was, that ever shall be, that even now is the fulfillment of the law of your being. The flame is your consciousness of continuity; it is the portion of the Spirit that is deathless, birthless, eternal.

In the flame you know that you have always existed and that you always will. In the flame is the merging of your soul and your Spirit in eternity. It is the matrix of the forever now that provides you with the understanding of the statement of the Christ "Before Abraham was, I AM."[1] In the flame you affirm and exalt the absolute perfection of your being.

The flame is a miniature sun. Only a sixteenth of an inch in h   e average man or woman, it is the magnet of
                ity in God. And lo, your individuality is an in-
                —as above, so below. As the flame is the I AM
                so it is the spark of life below. And so you

)

                self, the portion that is fully realized in

God, lives in Spirit; and that portion of the self not yet fully self-realized in God lives in the planes of Matter. That portion is the soul. And the flame, the lord or law of being, is the keeper of the soul even as the soul is intended to become the keeper of the flame. The soul is the sphere of identity that revolves around the sun center, the sacred fire. Dipping into the flame as the source of life in Matter, the soul also knows itself as God. But the soul's awareness includes the memory of past incarnations and interactions with other souls.

The soul is surrounded by an electronic forcefield that contains the cause, effect, record, and memory of those energies of karma which require balancing ere the soul can return to the plane of reality in the I AM Presence. This forcefield is called the electronic belt. It can be diagramed as the lower half of an egg positioned from the navel (or the solar plexus) to beneath the feet. You see, the lower portion of man and woman is surrounded by an energy field containing the entire records of the soul's involvement in the planes of Matter whose frequencies vibrate below the plane of mental awareness and hence are called subconscious. Thus man does not normally have an outer memory of the soul's experiences in previous lives, for these are kept below the surface of awareness in this lower portion of the etheric body.

The daily encounters of man and woman on the streets of life are in reality the unwinding of the cycles of karma—of positive and negative forces come full circle for the reckoning of the law of being. When people encounter past hatreds and animosities and the records of violent interchange, they sometimes, on contact with another person, find themselves seized with jealousy, anger, resentment, anxiety, or any of a multitude of negative reactions. Such experiences denote that pockets of energy misused in other lifetimes are coming to the surface of consciousness from

the plane of the subconscious for the restoration of balance
both within and among souls.

In the process, individuals must learn the art of self-mastery. They must learn to govern those energies in motion
that have recorded past indulgences in patterns of imper-
fection. Accidents, injuries, sudden illness, a turn of events
in business, in the household, or in the marriage may also
denote the descent of karma that is released through the
recycling of energy from the electronic belt.

When this occurs, O chelas of the white-fire core, know
that it is the testing of your soul and that it is time to enter
into the core of life that is the flame. Centered in the flame,
you can then challenge these negative spirals in the name
of your own Christ Self and call to the I AM Presence to release the flame into action and to pass the flame through the
subconscious for the transmutation of the cause and core of
every negative condition.

In so doing you will be practicing the art and science of
transmutation. You will be changing the frequency of energies disconnected from the source, so that they may be reunited with the source. And as these energies cycle back to
the source, your own soul awareness will follow. You will be
releasing energy locked in imperfect patterns, that it might
be sealed in patterns of perfection.

Each time a situation of imbalance occurs in your life, as
a chela on the path you must see it as an opportunity in the
present to right a wrong of the past. This is how you balance
karma. This is how you relieve the soul of the burden of the
synthetic image. Now life becomes a challenge! And you see
that you are what you are—a living flame—regardless of
what you think you are in those moments of encounter with
the accumulations of past energy sowings. And so the law is
fulfilled, "Whatsoever a man soweth, that shall he also reap."[2]

Be then the joyous reaper, knowing full well that as you cull the energies of karma into the flame, you will reap an abundant harvest of light. For locked in those energy coils is the life that is God. And when that misqualified energy comes into contact with the flame that is in your heart, it is requalified and sent forth to bless all life with perfect love, perfect wisdom, perfect power.

In our next release we will take up the study of the violet transmuting flame and what it can mean to the chela on the path of enlightenment.

Oh, be lightened in the light of the heart, whose servant I remain,

Morya

CHAPTER 5

_Chelas Centered in the Flame
and Those Who Would Be:_

Among masters I am known as a pragmatist in the truest sense of the word, for I am concerned with practicalities and with the exigencies of the hour. Mankind face a dilemma. It is a dilemma of the self, the society, and the civilization. The Darjeeling Council seeks answers to the dilemma. We probe the mind of God, and then we probe the mind of man. We are concerned with what will work—not with a pie-in-the-sky philosophy. We are concerned with what will work _now_ to stem the tide of world karma and the degradation of the image of the Christ as well as the image of the Divine Mother.

Chelas who knock on the door at Darjeeling are asked if they understand the urgency of world conditions and the crying need of the hour. If they have not yet gained that perspective, we recommend that they seek the disciplines of another retreat. For here at Darjeeling we offer a crash program in chelaship and initiation on the path for those who are willing to follow implicitly the demands of their own Christ Self and to respond with a flame that leaps and with eyes that sparkle with the kindling fires of soul discernment.

We send forth devotees of the Divine Mother. We train emissaries who will represent the Brotherhood and who will go forth into the large cities of the world to teach the way of the sacrifice of the self, as Saint Francis of old, for the greater glory of the Christ in all.

Come then; fear not to approach the fire blazing on the hearth here in the library of our retreat. Come now and meditate upon the flames, and see how the fiery salamanders dance to the music of the will of God that is the theme of your soul's reunion with the blueprint of your life, the grand design of destiny. See how the patterns blue and rose and gold woven in the Oriental rug recall the tapestry of the mind of God woven in your soul.

> So then take comfort
> In our cup of cheer—
> An elixir crystal clear
> Extended by angelic hands,
> Devas from angelic bands
> Who serve the diamond heart of Mary
> And welcome you to tarry.

May I play for you from *Moore's Irish Melodies* a song from my heart which I composed long ago for a loved one. I dedicate it now to all chelas of the sacred fire preparing for that transmutation and the forsaking of the outer, fading form for the inner, ever-blooming sunflower of the heart, "Believe Me, If All Those Endearing Young Charms." For the heart that has truly loved God never forgets the return current of that love reflected from the source of life. And so the soul, "as the sunflower, turns on her God, when he sets, the same look which she turn'd when he rose."[1]

Now, chelas of the will of God who would become

chelas of the ascended masters, with the tenderness of the heart of the will of God, I draw you into the folds of the garment of that will, that you might see that the crystal lining of the sapphire blue is flecked with a golden-pink hue—an intense love of the wisdom of God that inspires the Darjeeling masters to crack the whip of discipline. So great is our love for the soul of God in man that we would set you free to behold your immortal destiny.

There be some that come to our retreat for training, but their motives are not pure. They are self-seeking. They want power not to glory in God, but for the vainglory of the synthetic self which they refuse to surrender. They are told politely by the gatekeeper that those who enter must leave the slippers of the lesser self at the door. Those who are unwilling to take off the shoes of the shadowed self may not walk upon this hallowed ground.

It is time to enter the chamber designed with blue and gold motif where there is a screen and seats arranged in theater style. For to understand your path, your very personal path to salvation, you must have the perspective of your past and how you have created the present—both at personal and planetary levels. Come then; and let us see how we shall, in the magic of the flame, discover the designs of your soul destiny.

We enter the chamber now and take our places before a large semicircular screen on which there will be projected the experiences of other incarnations in the full dimensions that are portrayed from the akashic record. The group assembled here as I speak consists of unascended chelas—some of whom have an outer connection to the Retreat of the Resurrection Spiral in Colorado Springs, Colorado, and to Summit University in Santa Barbara, California. Others among the group are serving the will of God in their respective nations. These look forward to the day when the teachings of the ascended masters will be published in their language, that they might read and study in their outer, waking consciousness that which they receive here in their finer bodies during sleep.

One young couple taking their seats is accompanied by an unascended being of considerable attainment, of full stature and indeed recognized by the council. They will give birth to this soul in the not too distant future. I digress for a moment to point out this beautiful example wherein those who have united in love and in the sacred ritual of the marriage vow have been chosen by the Karmic Board even as they were chosen by this soul to give opportunity for an advanced lifestream to take embodiment in the service of humanity in the certainty of being reared in a home dedicated to the true law of the Lord.

Now scenes of life in ancient Thrace appear on the screen, and we find ourselves in the marketplace of a forgotten city in the land that is now Turkey. Two unascended masters walk midst the crowds unnoticed. The people are concerned with the activities of the day, with the purchase of food and supplies at the best prices, while the vendors carefully watch the passing of coins from hand to hand to see how much the day's business will bring. A group of devotees including some of the chelas now assembled in our retreat enters the marketplace. In this life they are mystics whose devotion is to the fire as it represents the one true God. Already they have borne the ridicule and the ostracism of their peers.

At the moment of their appearing, a peculiar astrological configuration aligns certain forces of hatred within the subconscious of the populace with an amalgamation of mass hatred focalized on astral planes. This interaction of forcefields in several dimensions of Matter we portray for the chelas, showing also the alignment of constellations, solar hierarchies, and "fixed" and "wandering" stars and how these energy fields amplify both the light and the darkness in mankind and cause the energizing of certain levels of karma in incarnations even prior to the ones now in focus on the screen.

Suddenly without warning, as if seized by a madness and a frenzy not entirely their own, certain individuals who seem to be at a random relationship to one another converge as a single entity. They act as a single unit—the mob—and with a single mind—the mass mind. They begin to pick up stones and hurl them at the devotees. The devotees are surrounded. Not terrified, but calmly centered in the flame that is the object of their worship, they shield their heads and their bodies. But to no avail.

The mob is brutal. With a desire for vengeance and a thirst for blood projected from the astral hordes, they descend upon the chelas until they are no more. Their souls take leave of that which remains of their finite forms, and the two unascended masters standing by raise the fohatic energies of their heart chakras to assist the souls in the transition. By karmic law they were not allowed to interfere with the circumstances that represented a converging of many forces and nature's demand for balance. Through their love and their mastery, they create a forcefield of light whereby the souls are taken safely to the etheric retreat of Pallas Athena over the island of Crete.

Now we roll back the drama on the screen so that all may examine the interplay of forces and the lines of karma that converged when the devotees first entered the marketplace. They see how they themselves in a much earlier period of earth's history, while engaged in the practice of a religion of darkness, were drawn into acts of fanaticism and untempered zeal which resulted in the death of those who retaliated that day in the forgotten city of ancient Thrace.

We review the scene in slow motion. I use the diamond that I wear on the index finger of my right hand to focus the action of the sacred fire on the screen. The violet ray that descends from the heart of my Presence is projected through the diamond and bursts forth as a thousand million flames on that scene on the screen. The chelas are on the edge of their seats as they watch the violet flame consume the cause and core, the record and memory—both in akasha and in their own subconscious.

The action of the violet flame intensifies in answer to my invocation made to the I AM Presence of each one: In the name of the Christ Self of the chelas, I invoke the fire of Almighty God to blaze forth the action of transmutation to change darkness into light—fear and hatred into love, envy into understanding, and vengeance into victory. As violet-flame angels from Zadkiel's retreat direct the energies of the flame, it forms coils of fire in the subconscious of each individual who was a party to this unfortunate interplay of energy.

Coils of fire are formed like the curly shavings that fall from planed wood. These coils rise and fall, rise and fall, intensifying the action of transmutation. And now they burst into a wide circle of energy and then return to the center. All of this is the action-formation of the fires of transmutation, flaming fire moving up and down and in and out; and then, following the circle of the cycles of individual karma in the electronic belt—a scrubbing action, a boiling action, a bubbling and a buoyant energy. Such is the diversity of the violet flame.

Scene by scene, step by step, the angels of the violet flame remove the record from the etheric body, the concepts from the mental body, the emotions from the feeling body, and the scars upon the physical matrix. Right before their very eyes, chelas of the will of God see what the glorious flame of God can do. They cheer. They applaud. And their bravos express the release of energy in their own hearts and a new freedom of the soul as this ancient record is cleared from their consciousness.

And now, in answer to the chelas' invocations to the violet flame, the fiery salamanders and the violet-flame angels, working hand in hand, retrace the record of that cycle when the lines of causation were drawn in the previous existence, which is also shown as chelas learn the lesson of blindly following the blind and of failing to invoke the wisdom of the Logos as a balance for the tyranny of the ego.

Next week we shall continue our investigations of the sacred fire and the flame of freedom—the violet energies that are the hallmark of the Aquarian age.

I AM for freedom through transmutation in God's will,

El Morya

Chelas Who Would Also Come to Darjeeling:

Those who attended the viewing in our retreat of the events at Thrace saw firsthand and for the first time in this incarnation the violet flame in action in the transmutation of the records of the past. Mankind living in the world today assume that recorded history is what it is and that it cannot be changed. They have not reckoned with the violet transmuting flame.

This flame is the energy of the sacred fire that is the gift of the Ascended Master Saint Germain to chelas of the will of God in this age. The dispensation for the release of the violet flame into the hands and use of the students in this century came forth from the Lords of Karma because Saint Germain went before that august body to plead the cause of freedom for and on behalf of mankind. He offered to the Lords of Karma the momentum of the violet flame garnered within his heart chakra and within his causal body as a momentum of light energy to be given to mankind that they might experiment with the alchemy of self-transformation through the sacred fire.

The violet flame has always been used in the retreats of

the Great White Brotherhood situated on the etheric plane—
the highest plane of Matter—where the ascended masters
preside, receiving only the most worthy chelas for instruction
and training in the way of initiation. Those who were found
worthy—adherents of the various religions, members of secret societies, communicants of the flame in the mystery
schools—were given the knowledge of the violet flame after
having proved themselves to be selfless as both receivers and
givers of freedom on the path of soul liberation.

Thus the violet flame was reserved for the privileged few
up until the time when Saint Germain came before the
Lords of Karma with the proposal to make the knowledge
and use of the violet flame available to all mankind. He
boldly stated before the Court of the Sacred Fire, arguing
as the advocate for earth's evolutions, that the violet flame
would revolutionize the human race and make of that race
a divine race of God-free beings.

Indeed, Saint Germain envisioned an "I AM race"[1] being raised up as the forerunners of the seventh root race
under the Great Divine Director. This blessed master of
freedom who had sponsored the birth of the nation called
the United States of America—this guardian of the Christ
consciousness who had walked the earth as the protector of
Mary and Jesus, this Saint Joseph, this Uncle Sam[2]—foresaw
the land of America from north to south, and eventually the
entire hemisphere, as the land that was destined to be a
haven for the Divine Mother and her progeny.

Inasmuch as he was destined to be the Master of the
Aquarian age and the God of Freedom to the earth, the
Lords of Karma agreed to the master plan with the following stipulation. First they would release the violet flame to a
certain nucleus of devotees in embodiment who would vow
at inner levels to use that flame honorably for the blessing

and the freedom of all life. If this experiment proved successful, they would allow the knowledge of the flame to be made available to the masses.

I am here to tell you that the dispensation could never have been granted for chelas to invoke this flame outside the retreats of the Great White Brotherhood had it not been for the fact that Saint Germain offered upon the altar of humanity the collateral of his own personal momentum of the energies of freedom garnered within his soul for thousands of years. For you see, when the Lords of Karma granted the dispensation through the intercession of this anointed one, they were fully aware that, given free will and given mankind's propensity to misuse that free will, it was altogether possible that certain numbers among mankind would misuse these sacred energies as they had done in the past in the days of ancient Lemuria and Atlantis. Were this to occur, someone would have to make up the difference.

Saint Germain understood this principle of cosmic law only too well. For the sake of the few and eventually the many who would make resplendent use of the violet flame, he was willing to forego and to sacrifice that portion of his momentum that would be misused and to chalk up that misuse as a necessary expenditure in the laboratory of mankind's consciousness. He was thereby in effect underwriting the experiments not only of the alchemists of the sacred fire with whom he had personally worked through the centuries, but also of the populace who would both use and misuse the alchemical fires ere coming into the enlightenment of the Christ mind and that centeredness in the Christ flame which is necessary for the responsible use of the violet flame.

Now you who are living in the advancing decades of the century are the beneficiaries of this legacy of Saint Germain bought with a price[3]—the overwhelming love of the Master

Saint Germain, whose love for you even before you took embodiment was such that he was willing to lay down a portion
of his life that you might live in the fullness of your individual God Self-awareness. Furthermore, you owe a debt of
gratitude to the early devotees who did in fact call forth the
flame with intense purity and devotion to the cause of mankind's freedom and therefore made possible the second phase
of the dispensation whereby you and countless others have
been given the knowledge of the violet flame in recent years.

Wherever you are, as you read my words you can begin
to experience the marvelous action of the violet fire coursing through your veins, penetrating the layers of the physical temple—the bloodstream, the nervous system, the brain
—pressing through the chakras, swirling through the etheric
body, passing over the pages of the written record of your
incarnations on earth. Line by line, letter by letter, the flame
—intelligent, luminous, directed by the mind of God—sets
free the energies, electron by electron, of all past misuses of
the sacred fire. And thus not one jot or tittle of the law of
karma shall pass until all be fulfilled[4] in the freedom of the
violet fire.

If you would have the benefit of this miraculous energy,
if you would be visited by the genie of the lamp of freedom,
the Master Saint Germain himself, you have but to make the
call. For the fiat of Almighty God has gone forth, and it is
cosmic law: The call compels the answer! But the call is a very
special call. It is not the demand of the human consciousness, but the command of your Real Self, your own true
being, the mediator between the I AM Presence and the
    ¹ Thus you declare:

                    ¬ame of the Christ Self and in the name of the
                    ∟l forth the energies of the sacred fire from the
                    ιy heart. In the name of the I AM THAT I AM,

I invoke the violet flame to blaze forth from the center of the threefold flame, from the white-fire core of my own I AM Presence, multiplied by the momentum of the blessed Ascended Master Saint Germain. I call forth that light to penetrate my soul and to activate my soul memory of freedom and the original blueprint of my soul's destiny. I call forth the violet transmuting flame to pass through my four lower bodies and through my soul consciousness to transmute the cause and core of all that is less than my Christ-perfection, all that is not in keeping with the will of God for my lifestream. So let it be done by the cloven tongues of the fire of the Holy Spirit[5] in fulfillment of the action of that sacred fire as above, so below. And I accept it done this hour in the full power of the living God who even now declares within my soul, 'I AM WHO I AM.'"

The violet flame comes forth from the violet ray, that aspect of the white light that is called the seventh ray. It is indeed the seventh-ray aspect of the Holy Spirit. Just as the sunlight passing through a prism is refracted into the rainbow of the seven color rays, so through the consciousness of the Holy Spirit the light of the Christ is refracted for mankind's use in the planes of Matter.

Each of the seven rays is a concentrated, activating force of the light of God having a specific color and frequency. Each ray can also manifest as a flame of the same color and vibration. The application of the flame results in a specific action of the Christ in body and soul, mind and heart. We shall consider the other six aspects of the sacred fire as our course unfolds.

Now let us examine what happens when the specific of the violet fire is applied to the recalcitrant conditions of the human consciousness. When, as an act of your free will, you make the call to the violet flame and you surrender these unwanted, untoward conditions into the flame, the fire instantaneously begins the work of breaking down particles of substance that are part of the mass accumulation of hundreds and even thousands of incarnations when in ignorance you allowed to register—through your consciousness, through your attention, thoughts and feelings, words and actions—all of the degrading conditions to which the human race is heir.

I trust that I need not enumerate the seemingly endless but altogether finite qualities of limitation thrust upon the ethers—projectiles of the carnal mind—that have filled the wide-open spaces between the electrons and the nuclei of the atoms with the densities of mankind's carnality. Believe it or not, this energy can be as hard as concrete or as sticky as molasses as it registers in all of the four lower bodies, causing mental recalcitrance, hardness of heart, and a lack of sensitivity to the needs of others and creating a dense mass that prevents the soul from receiving the delicate impartations of the Holy Spirit. So thick is the wall of mankind's density, of layer upon layer of their misuses of the sacred fire, that they don't even recognize the ascended masters as their liberators nor are they able to make contact with the blessed Christ Self, their own mediator of perfection who would confirm the reality of the ascended masters.

When the violet flame is invoked, it loosens the dense substance and passes through and transforms that darkness into light. Since every human condition is the perversion of a divine condition, line for line, measure for measure, the human consciousness is changed into the divine and the energy that was locked in pockets of mortality is freed to enter the sockets of immortality. And each time a measure of energy is freed, a measure of a man ascends to the plane of God-awareness.

As you begin to use the violet flame, you will experience feelings of joy, lightness, hope, and newness of life as though clouds of depression were being dissolved by the very sun of your own being. And the oppression of the very dark, dank energies of human bondage literally melts in the fervent heat of freedom's violet fires.

Lord Zadkiel, Archangel of the Seventh Ray, made certain that the chelas of the new age would understand the joyousness of the flame, and so he called it the violet singing flame. Indeed, this flaming presence causes the very atoms and molecules of your being to "sing" as they resume their normal frequency and are therefore brought into "pitch" with the keynote of your own lifestream. This keynote is the sounding of the chord of your own I AM Presence. And when, by the action of the violet flame, you free the energies of your four lower bodies to respond to that chord, the wonderful world of the microcosm moves in harmony with the grand Macrocosm of your I AM Presence and causal body.

The violet flame forgives as it frees, consumes as it transmutes, clears the records of past karma (thus balancing your debts to life), equalizes the flow of energy between yourself and other lifestreams, and propels you into the arms of the living God. Day by day you are ascending higher and higher in the planes of consciousness of your Christ Self as you use the scrubbing action of the violet flame and feel how the very walls of your mental body are scoured. You can think of this action in your desire body as the dunking of your emotions in a chemical solution of purple liquid that dissolves the dirt that has accumulated for decades about the latticework of your feeling world.

Every day in every way the violet flame flushes out and renews your body cells, the cells of your mind, and the 'globule' of your soul, polishing the jewel of consciousness until it glistens in the sunlight, dazzling as a pure molecule of being offered upon the altar of the sacred fire as an offering that is fitting for the Lord—your gift to God and man. And what better gift is there than the gift of selfhood? In reality, this is all that you have to offer. And so when you use the violet flame, you are laying down the impoverished self, the lesser self, that the self that is real might act to increase the blessings of God's consciousness worlds without end.

I recommend that you use the violet flame in the name and in the flame of Saint Germain.[6] And in his words I say to all who would be chelas of the will of God, *try*. For as the Master Alchemist has said, in the word "try" is the sacred formula of being: Theos = God; Rule = Law; You = Being; *Theos + Rule + You = God's Law Active as Principle within Your Being (TRY)*.[7]

Let the energies of the violet flame unlock your true self even as they sweep away the encrustations of the synthetic self. Let the violet flame work in you the works of God.

Until we meet again in Darjeeling, I AM

El Morya

Exponent of the Freedom of God's Will

CHAPTER 7

Chelas of Freedom's Will:

Will I AM: I AM the will of the flame. Have you transferred your allegiance to the Master of Freedom and the all-consuming violet flame? If fickle you must be—and I say this with a twinkle in my eye—then at least let the alternating current of your affection be the interplay of your devotion between the ascended masters known as the Chohans of the Rays! How I joy to behold the joy in the hearts of the devotees who discover the multiplication of the body of the Lord in the many ascended masters who have attained liberation through the fulfillment of the laws of the one true God and the entering-in to the flame of the only begotten Son.

You who have discovered the flame within have at last discovered the Christ as the signet of your true being. This Christ flame is the sign, the living proof, that you are a son, a daughter, of God. Let no man take thy crown.[1] Let no man take from thee this appellation. Behold, thou art the Christ forevermore![2] The Christ flame is your claim to individuality in God, to immortality—to the perpetuation of selfhood beyond the mortal frame and beyond the planes of time and space.

The Master of Galilee came to extol that flame, to set the example of a life lived in the flame. So you also have come called by God to be an example to the age, to set your mark upon the page, the mark of the life that is lived in God, of the love that is willed in Christ. As you claim the potential of the Christ flame, as you affirm your individuality in God, know that you do so with the absolute authority of your own I AM Presence and of the Holy Spirit. For he said, "This is my body which is broken for you."[3]

The fragments of the light body of the eternal Logos, the same "Light which lighteth every man that cometh into the world,"[4] are throughout the creation the fullness of the living Christ whom God, because he so loved the world,[5] gave to every son and daughter. Understand that in the gift of life, the threefold flame, the Lord God literally gave to all of his children the flaming essence of the Only Begotten that through conformity with this essence the world might be saved from sin, disease, and death.

"In him we live and move and have our being, for we are also his offspring."[6] We are the ascended masters. We are the Chohans (Lords) of the Rays. Each of the seven rays that is the fulfillment of an aspect of the Christ consciousness is ensouled by an ascended master who has graduated from the schoolrooms of earth, ascended into the Presence of the I AM THAT I AM, and stands as the teacher of the way of self-mastery on a particular ray, or radiance, of the Christ mind.

And so as Chohan of the First Ray, I teach the law of the will of God and the mastery of energy through the throat chakra in the science of the spoken word.[7] Lord Lanto, the Master of Wisdom who taught wisdom's way in ancient China, teaches the path of attainment through enlightenment, definition, and dominion in the crown chakra. Paul the Venetian, who was embodied as the Italian artist Paolo Veronese, is the Lord of the Third Ray of divine love. His chelas learn the art of keeping the flame through the discipline of love and the mastery of the flow of creative forces through the heart chakra.

The Chohan of the Fourth Ray is the Master Serapis Bey—a Spartan if I ever saw one—whose fiery determination has saved many a soul from the mush of self-indulgence. His chelas reflect the fierceness of their master as they are immovable in their dedication to purity focused as the Mother light in the base-of-the-spine chakra. Hilarion, devotee of truth and scientist of the new age, was embodied as Saint Paul. As Chohan of the Fifth Ray, he reveals the path of mastery through science, truth, healing, and the immaculate vision of God through the third-eye chakra.

Beloved Nada, our Lady Chohan, who was embodied as a lawyer in defense of cosmic justice, serves as the Lord of the Sixth Ray, showing the way of Jesus, the way of humble service and ministration that adorns the talents of others with the rose of selflessness and unlocks their creative potential through the mastery of energy in motion in the solar-plexus chakra. Her motto is the golden rule, "Do unto others as you would have them do unto you."[8]

Nada's chelas pave the way for the golden age of Aquarius under Saint Germain. The Lord of the Seventh Ray, who is the Master of Alchemy, teaches not only the uses of the energies of freedom and the spirit of liberty, but also the way of the alchemical ritual as a necessary component of soul liberation. His ritual is alive with meaning. In his retreat in Transylvania he unveils the symbology of the ritual of the atom and the formulae of the cycles for the release of God's energy in manifestation in man.

All mankind are born to serve and to master the self on

one of the seven rays. Their first guru, then, after the Christ
Self, who is the true teacher of each man and woman, is the
Chohan of the Ray on which they serve. Therefore, those
who would be chelas, those who would pursue the path of
soul liberation, will be happy to know that there are seven
distinct paths of Christhood, that one of these paths is best
fitted to your soul personality and inner calling, and that a
second will complement the first. And so you might say that
on the seven rays you have a major and a minor concentration of study and application in the law of becoming the
Christ.

Now it is your supreme privilege to define in your world
and in your life the path that you will pursue on the home-
ward way. As you learn more of the ascended masters and
their teachings, as you play their taped dictations given at
quarterly conferences, as you read and meditate upon their
words, you will begin to identify the positioning of your soul
on one of the paths of the seven rays.

Realize, too, that it is the requirement of the ascension
that you garner a sufficiency of the white light in your four
lower bodies; for the white light is the source of all of the
color rays. It is the fiery core of the flame out of which is
spun the wedding garment.[9] Your momentum of the white
light is the means whereby you magnetize the flame of the
ascension in the hour of your victory.

In order to achieve the mastery of the white light, you
must have a certain mastery on all of the seven rays; for as
you master the rays, they lead you back to the center of the
white light, back to the prism of the Christ consciousness
whence they came. Moreover, it is impossible to gain mastery on one of the seven rays without this mastery carrying
over through the oneness of the white-fire core to other
aspects of the Christ consciousness. Nevertheless, your high

calling as a son or daughter of God which we term the sacred labor—which involves the perfecting of the talents that God has placed within your soul—will be achieved on the ray of your major with the support of your minor. All else will be an adornment of that central fiery purpose.

Every soul by free will elects the path of his own ascension. Your soul has already chosen and developed a considerable momentum on the ray of its destiny. This occurred while the soul was yet cycling within the spheres of the causal body prior to incarnation in the planes of Matter. The causal body of every son and daughter of God reflects this larger momentum of concentration on the chosen ray.

Thus you will hear chelas of the ascended masters referring to one another as being "on the first ray" or "on the second ray" or "on the fifth ray." Or you may hear them say, "So-and-so has a great momentum on the fourth ray and on the seventh ray." This is good. For when you identify God as a flame and as the personality of the flame, it is good to identify friends and chelas alike as these identify with the flame rather than according to the outer personality or to the momentums of negative karma.

Learn then, O chelas of the sacred fire, to behold one another as living flames. Learn to see the soul and the intent of the soul. Learn to judge by the motive of the heart. Learn to accept one another for what you are in truth and in reality—exponents of the Christ endued with power from on high, imbued with love from the heart of the Christ, exuding the wisdom of the flame whose origin is the universal mind of God.

This week I ask you to call in the name of your own Christ Self to each of the seven Chohans of the Rays to invoke their assistance on the path. You may ask to be taken to each of their retreats on successive nights.[10] On Sunday

night before retiring, you may make the following call,
adapting it for each of the subsequent evenings of the week:
"In the name of the Christ, my own Real Self, I call to the
heart of the I AM Presence and to the angel of the Presence
to take me in my soul and in my soul consciousness to the
retreat of Paul the Venetian in southern France. I ask to
receive the instruction of the law of love and to be given the
formula for the victory of the love flame within my heart.
And I ask that all information necessary to the fulfillment of
my divine plan be released to my outer waking consciousness as it is required. I thank thee and I accept this done in
the full power of the risen Christ."

On Monday evening you should make the call to be
taken to the Retreat of God's Will in Darjeeling for your four
lower bodies to be charged and recharged with the will of
God and the blueprint for your fulfillment of that will. On
Tuesday evening ask to be taken to the retreat of Hilarion
over the Island of Crete to be taught the way of truth, the
revelations of truth, and the true revelations of Jesus Christ
the age under the Apostle Paul, the Ascended Master
Hilarion.

On Wednesday evening make the call to be taken to the
retreat of Jesus in Arabia, where Nada will instruct you in
the mastery of the emotions for the flow of peace and the
anchoring of the flame of the Prince of Peace to all mankind. On Thursday evening ask to be taken to the temple at
Luxor to join the candidates for the ascension as they hear
the word of Serapis Bey and learn of the Redeemer that
is within the flame of the heart.

On Friday night call to be taken to the Cave of Symbols,
the retreat of Saint Germain on the North American continent, so that you may be saturated with the violet flame focused there and so that you may begin to master the ritual

of the atom for the Aquarian Age. On Saturday evening be certain to meditate on the Grand Teton as you ask to be taken to the Royal Teton Retreat to learn the way of wisdom and the lessons of illumined action for the precipitation of the Christ consciousness under Lord Lanto.

May I quote the words of the World Teacher Jesus the Christ as I ask you to follow this ritual of calls nightly over the weeks when you are reading my *Pearls of Wisdom:* "This do in remembrance of me."[11]

In remembrance of the Great Guru, I send forth greetings from Darjeeling borne from my heart to your own on the winds of the Holy Spirit.

Morya

_____

CHAPTER 8

Chelas Who Would Become Messengers of the Gods:

Mercury is a planet of stalwart souls who have entered the fiery core of the discipline of the law, whose concentrated energies make them quick-footed and quick-minded.[1] Thus the God Mercury, depicted with winged sandals and with the wings of the mind, is the archetype of the messenger of the gods who transmutes the cloven hoof and the horns of the god Pan—one of the many disguises of Satan.

Chelas on the path must know the way. Jesus said, "Whither I go ye know, and the way ye know." Yet Thomas asked, "Lord, we know not whither thou goest; and how can we know the way?" The reply of the Christed one in every age must be "I AM the way."[2] For he understands, because he has realized the God Self as his true identity, that this God Self, whose name is I AM, is the way. And thus when he affirms, "I AM the way," it is understood that he is saying, "God in me is the way."[3]

I AM goal-fitting chelas to become representatives of hierarchy in the new age. Indeed, our representatives bring in the new age by exchanging the old man for the new.[4] I would transfer to my chelas the momentum of my attainment in the mercury diamond-shining mind of God. For I, too, have come under the tutelage of the God Mercury; and thus I have become a transmitter of the will of God, stepping down the energies of that will for lesser evolutions in many systems of worlds.

Being is electronic. Therefore another name for the I AM Presence is the Electronic Presence. Just as you have been taught to visualize the I AM Presence as the flaming identity of God surrounded by spherical rings comprising what is known as the causal body, so you may also visualize that being which is your God-reality as a galaxy of light, a spiritual forcefield of tremendous cosmic power, wisdom, and love that is your very own.

Cosmic consciousness is the realization of self as the galaxy of light which declares from the very center of the atom of being, "I AM WHO I AM." Forevermore down the corridors of eternity the formula of beness echoes as the mathematics of the spoken Word: I AM WHO I AM. This, the very first equation of being and consciousness, is the foundation of your alchemical experiment that leads to the fullness of that life which is God.

I say, then, come with me. Expand the field of the mind. Tread the cosmic highways which I have trod which lead to the throne of Almighty God. If you are to become a messenger of the gods, you must get out of the finite consciousness and the confines of the mortal dilemma. You must be able to see beyond the finite self, beyond your Lilliputian world, and by co-measurement perceive the vastness of the plan—the vastness of God's being which you can make your own.

A journey to the center of the sun to expand the horizon

of heart and mind: this I propose for chelas who will make
the call, who will not fear to enter the fire of the heart or to
be retained in the capsule of my identity—a rocket sufficient for the journey. Therefore, make the call and come.
Make haste, for we leave at the midnight hour from the
Temple of God's Will. Like the little prince of Saint-Exupéry,
you will study lifewaves of other systems of worlds. And you
will see against the backdrop of the childlike innocence of
your own soul how evolutions in Matter have confined
themselves to pockets of consciousness that make them use-
less until they choose to evolve into a dimension of being
that includes an awareness of other parts of life as equal to
their own.

In order for mankind to break the cycles of a dead and
dying world, in order for mankind to refrain from iden-
tifying with the spirals of disintegration and to ride instead
the spirals of integration that lead to the source of life, they
must be given a new perspective of life. This comes through
the conceptualization of co-measurement whereby the measure of a man is measured against the measure of a cosmos.

Look up into the stars and know that there identity has
realized selfhood in God. Know that the stars in the firmament of God's being reflect the glory of the "elder days of
Art"[5]—of those forgotten yesteryears when sons and daughters of God, members of the early root races of this and
other systems of worlds, triumphed in the law of the Logos,
overcame time and space, and ascended to the plane of
God-reality where they sustain the starry body and the starry
consciousness of concentrated fire, leaving a counterpart in
Matter to mark the point of victory. Stars are markers of
those who have overcome. Thus you, too, can say: "We shall
overcome. Earth shall become a star. The evolutions of
Terra shall be free."

It is time to seriously consider the nature of the expansion of the teachings of the ascended masters. It is necessary to understand how you figure in the hierarchy of unascended chelas serving the will of God. Those who would be messengers of the ascended masters, whom mankind have identified as the gods and goddesses of ancient mythology, at times erroneously attributing to them human qualities, must learn to communicate with mankind in their present level of development.

When you speak to a child, you speak simply, clearly, and in the vocabulary of the child. Thus there are times when we address mankind in the vernacular of the day and there are times when we dress somewhat in the fashion of the day; yet we preserve the word of the Logos when speaking directly to the soul in the classical language of the Spirit known to every soul even as we preserve the mode of the seamless garment of light.[6] To every plane of being we come, and we address ourselves to the frequency of consciousness in the state of becoming whole. We admonish our chelas to do likewise—to meet the consciousness of humanity where it is today, to meet the needs of the hour, to answer the questions that demand answers, and to touch on those subjects of the law that are of universal concern.

Here and there in the wilderness of mankind's consciousness you will hear our voice speaking through teachers, prophets, statesmen, or the philosopher of the common man. You must take care that the fire you bring does not scorch the wings of the aspirant set for his first solo flight, for the fire that you bring is to warm the heart and to melt hardness of heart. Let the wax of the candle of self be consumed because you have kindled a flame that can be self-contained.

Let it be clear to those who are concerned lest they become the slave of the master, that we will not permit it unless

it be by your free will. You need become only the slave of
the law of your own being, the slave of your own reality.
Take care, then, that when in fear you deny the teacher as
the master and when you reject the master as the teacher,
you do not sink into the slavery of your own carnal mind.
This is unwise dominion.

To allow oneself to be dominated by one's own karma
or the cycles of one's astrology—this is indeed the folly of
those who have witlessly removed themselves from the path.
They might as well have plunged from the narrow pass of
Himalayan heights into the abyss of nihilism. To preserve
the self above the teacher and above the law is to deny the
law of one's own reality with which the teacher is always one.
Each day you choose whose slave you shall become. I pray
that you choose wisely.

We send forth a thrust for a purpose, that the rocket of
self may be thrust into the galaxy of God-reality. The energy
of our thrust is a grant that must be met in equal intensity
by your own determination. Thus when the energy of your
thrust for a cosmic purpose becomes equal to the thrust deposited in your account, your soul will break away from the
gravitational pull of the untransmuted karma of a planet
and her people.

Day by day you are required to invoke from the central
sun of your own being energy that is sufficient for the overcoming of the gravitational pull of your own untransmuted
karma. When you feel weighted down, pulled by the emotions of the mass consciousness, and you find yourself in
sympathy with the woes of the world, you must be alert to
detect that the thrust of the light of your auric forcefield is
on the wane. It is then that the burden you carry, which is
indeed the karmic weight of many lifestreams, must become
a burden of light.

Only through the use of the sacred alchemical formula of the Master Saint Germain can you accomplish the transmutation whereby the burden of darkness becomes the burden of light of which Jesus spoke when he said: "Come unto me, all ye that labour and are heavy laden, and I will give you rest. . . . For my yoke is easy, and my burden is light."[7] Indeed, when you possess the sacred formula keyed in the word "try," you, too, can say, "My yoke is easy."

The yoke of karma which you are allowed to carry for and on behalf of mankind is measured by your ability to demonstrate the laws of alchemy. The demonstration of these laws must begin—and there is no other way—with your invocation to the violet flame. I therefore urge all who are in earnest on the path of chelaship to procure a set of *Prayers, Meditations, and Dynamic Decrees for the Coming Revolution in Higher Consciousness*[8] and to develop a concentrated momentum of application to the law of the violet flame.

When I come to the door and knock, I expect to be greeted by a chela wearing the royal robe of purple. If you would bid me enter your house, then prepare the forcefield. Let it be supercharged with the fires of freedom; for I would breathe the pure air of freedom—not the musty odor of the decaying human consciousness. If you would be a chela of Morya or of one of the chohans of the rays, then I say, let your house be a house of light. Let your aura be filled with the joyous fires of freedom. Roll out the violet carpet, and see how the masters will come to teach you and to lead you in the paths of righteousness (the right use of the law) for his name's sake.[9]

Now then, chelas of the will of God, alchemists of the sacred fire, I would have you experiment in the garnering of a momentum of reality, a concentrated focus of the sacred fire sufficient for the breaking-away of your soul from the forcefields of unreality. I would have you break the bonds of mortality. I have interceded, that you might receive the energies of our thrust. Let us see how many chelas will match that thrust by invocation and by fervent prayer.

I shall return. Watch and pray.

Morya

CHAPTER 9

Chelas Garnering a Thrust for a Purpose:

I have said that being is electronic. Your Electronic Presence is a sun center of whirling energies of light garnering consciousness. It is a fire infolding itself.[1] It is a magnetic forcefield drawing unto itself pure being, pure selfhood, cycle by cycle increasing a point of God Self-awareness, the awareness of being as the fiery nucleus of life.

Here below in the planes of Matter life is also electronic. Man is a forcefield, complex, of whirling energies, molecules of Matter. He is a chemical formula all his own composed of many chemical elements. Man is a physical equation. Obedient to the laws of physics, he moves in time and space. Yet the soul is not bound by time and space; neither is it confined in its expression to the laws of chemistry and physics. The soul is an electron of the Great Central Sun of being. Orbiting around the I AM Presence, the soul is the electron that has the option of electing to do God's will.

You who have elected to do that will have called yourselves chelas, and you are called by us chelas of the ascended masters. The path that you are following is in reality the path of the law that governs the electron in its orbit around the sun that is the I AM Presence. Those who are not on the path, whether consciously or unconsciously, are no longer free to move in and around and through the energies of the I AM Presence. They have not overcome the gravity of the mass consciousness. Their souls have not taken flight.

To be free to respond to the initiations of the path, you must be free from the magnetism of mankind's carnal-mindedness. "For to be carnally minded is death, but to be spiritually minded is life and peace."[2] Indeed, there can be no chela and no path unless the electron of being is free to elect to return to the center of God. Chelaship is the way of transition from the plane of the mass consciousness to the heights of God consciousness. Unless he can garner enough light in the aura of self to keep him free to orbit around his own sun center, the chela, by definition, is not the chela.

You then have a responsibility; and that responsibility is to keep yourselves so filled with light that at any hour of the day or night you are found free moving, a free agent of the sacred fire—not bound by your own sense of limitation or the limitation which others would impose upon you. You must be free to accept the limitless reality of your being. You must not allow anyone to take from you the freedom to be unlimited in your God Self. God made you free, and you must defend the law of your being and your freedom to create after the image and likeness[3] of your own God-reality.

Just as you must garner the necessary thrust of light to preserve the freedom of your soul, to preserve your soul in freedom, so the planet as a whole must retain that thrust of light that will keep it in orbit not only around the physical sun center of this solar system, but also around the spiritual sun that is the source of life for all lifewaves in the system. Each one who is able to sustain the thrust of light required to keep himself free becomes a candidate for the garnering of energies necessary to keep the planet free.

The weight of world karma has never been greater. The Divine Mother intercedes before the Court of the Sacred Fire on behalf of the children of God that the descent of their own karma might not destroy the very platform of their evolution. As Thoreau said, "What is the use of a house if you haven't got a tolerable planet to put it on?" So we say, what is the use of the path of initiation if the planetary platform can no longer sustain its evolutions?

Therefore, the path of initiation is drawn with two parallel lines. The first is man attaining self-mastery in the microcosm of his being, and the second is man attaining self-mastery in the Macrocosm of the planetary body and consciousness. Chelas who have garnered the thrust of energy necessary to sustain the first line of initiation are given the opportunity to sustain the second.

So many upon the planet earth ignore the laws of God and their own opportunity to make any advancement whatsoever along spiritual lines that it is a requirement of the great law that the few in every age carry the weight of planetary karma in order that the many might find opportunity for overcoming both in the present and in the future because the planetary platform has been preserved.

Jesus the Christ was the saviour of the world because in the moment of victory he held the balance for all mankind. This means that the thrust of light that he garnered within his aura was sufficient to hold the balance for the entire weight of the sins of the world. Because he held that balance, you and all mankind have the opportunity for evolution here and now.

Now it is your turn. Your time has come. Now you can join the forces of your light momentum to that of the saviour of the world and you can declare, "In Christ I AM [God in me is] the saviour of the world!" and thereby draw to yourself the energies of salvation that are for the preservation of a planet and a people.

As long as you retain the awareness of who you really are and what you really are and where you really are, this true awareness of selfhood will enable you to maintain an expanded forcefield of consciousness that will attract grids of light from the heart of your own I AM Presence. And thereby you will become a blazing sun center of light here below in the planes of Matter just as you are in reality in the planes of Spirit.

If you would preserve the path of initiation for yourself and your offspring, then you have a vested interest in preserving the planetary platform. And as you look upon the world today, no matter what your perspective, you can truthfully say all is not well with mankind.

Those who elect to be electrons of God must move among mankind, that the light of their auras might be absorbed by souls in need of light. Each soul who learns to garner a thrust for the preservation of the Macrocosm must also unite with other souls whose auric field has a similar intensity. Hierarchy requires nuclei of souls who will band together for the meshing of their electronic fields for the sake of reinforcing one another's light body, one another's determination in the will of God.

This requires sacrifice—the sacrifice of the human consciousness. Hierarchy has sponsored many uplift movements. We have founded organizations before, and always there have been those factors of differences in the human personality which chelas have allowed to come between them and their cosmic purpose. "All your strength is in your union"[4]—first with the God Self and then with one another.

The principles of geometry must be understood when

you determine to unite for hierarchy. You must not allow
gossip, misunderstanding, or personal idiosyncrasies to stand
between you and your service. We do not need splintered
groups, fragmented or fractioned energies. We need a body
of devotees all for one and one for all.

You must understand, then, that one of the early initiations on the path is intended to prove whether or not the
chela can get along with other chelas. The chela who sepa-
rates himself bodily from the body of devotees serving the
Christ and removes himself into an ivory tower of spiritual
pride and self-righteousness is not eligible for membership
in the Great White Brotherhood. Brotherhood means "I AM
my brother's keeper."[5] This is the byword of overcomers.
Having overcome, they have said, "We are responsible for
those who have yet to overcome."

And therefore long ago the fraternity of the Great White
Brotherhood was formed. It is a fraternity of ascended and
unascended beings, of those who have overcome and of those
who are yet overcoming. And the term "white" signifies that
they are garnering the thrust of energy necessary for a cosmic purpose and for the fulfillment of that purpose in an
entire planetary body and in an entire system of worlds. Our
thrust cannot be content to remain within the confines of
the single electron. We trust that our thrust is great enough
to thrust the entire world into the white-fire core of being,
into the fiery blueprint of the inner geometry.

How can we expand the ascended masters' teachings or
the ascended masters' activity when our chelas bicker among
themselves about the form of services or about what decrees
should be given or about methods of outreach? Our chelas
must present a united front to the world. Our chelas must
show that the knowledge of ascended-master law leads to
love, unity, and above all, a caring and a compassion for one

another. Chelas must be living proof that ascended-master law meets every need—human and divine.

Remember this and listen well: If you can't get along with or serve your fellowman or your fellow chela on the path, then you won't get along with or serve the ascended masters. And so we withdraw from those who call themselves chelas but who fail in their service to and with each other.

Then there is always the chela who says sanctimoniously to another chela on the path, "Well, I love your Christ Self, but I can't stand your human." They presuppose that they understand which is which. They look at the chela and they see the human. I say, look again and behold in his place the master who declared, "Inasmuch as ye have done it unto one of the least of these my brethren, ye have done it unto me."[6]

Can you look at me squarely in the eye and tell me that you always know when the human consciousness is acting and when it is the master working through a fellow chela to test the threshold of your pride, your irritation? We do not need to appear to the chela to test his soul. We have only to use another chela to determine what is the level of sacrifice. How much of the self are you willing to surrender in order to retain the privilege of working side by side with those whose devotion to our flame may be far beyond your own?

When the chelas of the ascended masters will demonstrate their unity in the flame, then they will see how their combined thrust of light energy will expand the work and bring the planet into the golden age.

I shall come again to bring you signs of the path of your soul's overcoming. Be of good cheer. The ascended masters have overcome the world.[7]

Morya

CHAPTER 10

Chelas Suspended in the
Grid of Cosmic Consciousness:

See yourself jumping on the trampoline of God's mind. See yourself bouncing on the grid of energy that is pure intelligence—translucent, glistening cords intermeshed for the interplay of identities in and through the mind that is God. Yes, see yourself turning somersaults in your etheric body, performing the gymnastics of mind and soul that lead to total self-identification with the being and consciousness that is God.

I would move the mind of the chela into cosmic dimensions of selfhood, and thus I give a visualization to stretch your imagination. Let the ball of identity bounce from the confines of the flesh. Let it leave the body and return at will, as a ball[1] bouncing across the miles of Terra, moving as a nucleus of energy over the surface of the earth, then bouncing into outer space, spanning the space between planets. Let yourself bounce across the cosmic highways and in and out of the planes of Matter. So the ball of self is free to explore a cosmos; and though a million light-years away on etheric planes of consciousness, it can return in the twinkling of an eye to body temple and body consciousness evolving on Terra.

Free your mind to be everywhere in the consciousness of God. Free your mind to roam his mind. Free your desires to merge with God's desiring to be, and let your desires take on the desires of infinity. Deity sires creation. And the siring is the desiring of God to be more of himself. Thus the soul desires to be more of God, and rightfully so. How to achieve that goal is the subject of chelaship.

To be a chela on the path of realizing a cosmic selfhood, you must train the mind to be free, to explore, and to discover self on many planes of being, to move with dexterity up and down the ladder of God's cosmic consciousness as the astronaut preparing for the walk in outer space, inner space. So you must become accustomed to penetrating life beyond the planet and then returning to the plane of practicality, of physicality, where you come to grips with keeping your accounts in order, keeping your house neat and clean, keeping your schedules, and keeping the balance in your relationship of employer and employee, husband and wife, father and son, mother and daughter.

The farther you would go from your point of individuality in Matter, the more tethered you must be to that point. Self-discipline in the law of everyday living, obedience to the laws of God and man, exactness in detail, precision in the precepts of the Logos and of the Mother—these prepare your soul and your consciousness to expand and to reach out for the coordinates of the higher geometry of selfhood. Moving from plane to plane, the requirements of the law are more demanding; and thus the mastery of the self here below is necessary for the mastery of the self in the vast beyond.

Preparation is all. Prepare to meet thy God. Prepare to

meet the flaming yod. Prepare to enter into the within. Prepare for the fling from the within to the without. God is all. He is the All-in-all. The path of the chela is the path whereby the all becomes the All.

I have spoken of the atoms of selfhood reinforcing one another in time and space whose light bodies are a momentum for the balance of planetary karma. I have spoken of the need for nuclei of souls gathering unto themselves skeins of light, reinforcing one another's light momentum. The hallowed circle of the AUM is formed as chelas of the ascended masters assemble to affirm God-victory now, to affirm with him: "I AM the light of the world: he that followeth me [the light of the Christ which I AM] shall not walk in darkness, but shall have the light of life."[2]

The voice of the master echoes in the memory of every devotee of the flame: "I say unto you, if two of you shall agree on earth as touching any thing that they shall ask, it shall be done for them of my Father which is in heaven. For where two or three are gathered together in my name, there am I in the midst of them."[3] This is the hallowed circle of the AUM.

Chelas must magnetize one another in the flame of God. Chelas must come together for service beneath his rod. In every city where there are found chelas of the will of God, let them come together in the master's name. Let them come together to agree upon earth that the light of the eternal Christos shall be victorious in this age and that there shall be an imploding and an exploding of that light in the hearts of all mankind. Even as the Christ comes into each heart arrayed in his immortal light body, let the gathering of the elect be the gathering of electrons to welcome the Lord Christ in the midst of the circle of the AUM.

Many years ago the fiat went forth from Lord Maitreya,

the representative of the Cosmic Christ, that invocations offered unto Almighty God and the heavenly hosts in the name of the Christ and in the name of the I AM Presence would be answered by the power of the ten thousand-times-ten thousand. This means that every invocation given in the power of the spoken Word unto the Lord, or *law,* of your being is multiplied by cosmic forces, and the earth receives the light impact of that call one hundred million times its original release.

This geometric formula is also multiplied by the square of the number of individuals who come together to give invocations in the name of the I AM Presence. Whereas the individual who decrees alone (albeit *all one* with God the I AM Presence) has the momentum of one, and although one is indeed a majority with God, when two or three come together in the name of the Christ, the light-action of the two is squared to the momentum of four, the light-action of the three is squared to the momentum of nine, and so forth, until the light-action of the ten is squared to equal one hundred and the one hundred is squared to equal ten thousand. This is the multiplication of the Lord's body and the geometrization of his consciousness on earth as it is in heaven.

And so by cosmic law, chelas of the will of God and of the ascended masters ought not to let any thing, any one, or any circumstance deter them from coming together on a regular basis for the giving-forth of their energies in invocations and decrees to the sacred fire for the alleviation of world conditions—for the transmutation of pain and sorrow, death and dying. As those who come together each week consecrate their energies in service to the ascended masters, their counterparts among the angelic hosts gather to blend their voices with the unascended chelas and to multiply the momentum as below, so above.

Those who have been a part of the group decree sessions that have been held over the years in many cities across this land and throughout the world can know with a certainty that by constancy in the flame you have kept the light momentum necessary for the holding of the balance in your communities, in your states, in your nations, and even on a world scale. Now in view of the report from the Karmic Board which has gone forth to the Keepers of the Flame in a recent dictation given by the Great Divine Director, I ask that chelas associated with our groups make a pledge to Saint Germain and to the Lords of Karma to come together in group decree sessions on a regular basis without fail and that you set aside a morning, an afternoon, or an evening each week which you never miss except in the case of a dire emergency.

In view of world conditions—the threat of war in the Middle East, the threat of mass starvation and even social, economic, and physical cataclysm—the legions of light from cosmic levels have come forth to form nuclei of energy, forcefields through which an intense release of energy from the spiritual to the material universe can occur. These forcefields are being set up over every focus of the ascended masters, wherever there are chelas who gather together in the name of the Christ for service to hierarchy and to the cause of freedom. These grids of light are set up to match the pattern of your own forcefield below, and the geometry is exact.

Therefore we must know whom we can count upon at every hour of the day or night. Thus whether you are alone in your service or (preferably) are joining the ranks of lightbearers, will you write down the day, the hour, and the place of your coming together—marking the time when your invocations will begin and end—so that hierarchy may implement this plan for the reinforcement of your invocations and decrees and for the uniting of these nuclei by lines of force, by the thread of contact, by the web of light that has been called the antahkarana of world servers.

This antahkarana, an energy field of the mind of God itself, is designed to connect hearts of light the planet round so that at any hour of the day or night children of the light may tune into the Lord's hosts, to legions of light, and to the momentum of the Christ consciousness garnered in the individual and the group matrix. And every soul who commits himself to be a part of this chain of hierarchy may also find himself strengthened in an hour of testing by the unified consciousness of all chelas on the path.

Only those who sustain a momentum of service and keep the flame of their hour will remain a part of this chain of oneness. Those who fail in their commitment will find that by cosmic law the angelic hosts will withdraw and for their lack of constancy the grid will dissolve. It would be best for you to commit yourself to the minimum service of which you are capable, that which by the measure of your past performance you are certain of maintaining. Then you can and should augment your service whenever possible. Thus you will always be certain of keeping your promise to the hosts of the Lord. Do not keep them waiting; for they, too, have commitments, and they wait upon the Lord their God as flaming spirits[4] tending the altars of the Most High according to cosmic cycles that are for the measuring of increments of eternity.

The giving of Mother Mary's Scriptural Rosary for the New Age, which the Blessed Mother dictated to our messenger, and "Watch With Me," Jesus' Vigil of the Hours[5] is indeed of utmost importance in sustaining a planetary force-field of light as well as the nuclei sun centers. These, together with daily invocations to the hierarchies of light and the flames of God as they are given in your *Prayers, Meditations, and Dynamic Decrees for the Coming Revolution in Higher*

Consciousness, produce the action that the great law requires for the holding of the balance in time of personal and planetary transition.

Of such import has been the coming-together of devotees of light down through the ages that when The Summit Lighthouse was founded, I set the pattern of the quarterly conferences for the anchoring of the cycles of the year. By coming together four times a year to give and receive, chelas of the ascended masters render an imcomparable service to the Great White Brotherhood. If you could behold our quarterly conferences from the inner planes, you would observe how the chelas build the forcefield in the physical plane by their devotions and by their oneness and how hierarchy lowers a grid that is the mandala for that class in the etheric plane over the physical place where the class is held.

The mandala is like a snowflake—unique in its design, never seen before, never to appear again. This geometric design suspended over the group is the focal point in which the energies of the group coalesce to magnetize, as a magnet of light, the releases of the ascended masters that are planned by the Karmic Board for that particular conference. Each lecture that is scheduled and each dictation that is given fills in a portion of the mandala, and the application of the students intensifies the action of the sacred fire that can be released to the planet.

Our conferences are held for the turning of the cycles of the year—winter solstice, spring equinox, summer solstice, and autumn equinox. The physical changes occur prior to the conference and the light released from the hierarchies of the sun at the change of the seasons is then expanded by ascended and unascended beings serving together at the conferences for the fulfillment of a cosmic purpose on earth as it is in heaven.

Whenever possible, you should seize the opportunity to attend such a conference. What's more, you should make possible the impossible through the alchemy of invocation to your own God Being. Not only are these conferences the most important experience of a lifetime in terms of the expansion of consciousness and the transmutation of untold substance in your world, but your willingness to serve as a coordinate on earth for the hierarchies of light will earn for you a momentum of good karma that you can ill afford to be without.

God needs man and man needs God. This is the law of the hallowed circle of the AUM. And when you find yourself standing in that circle, ever-widening, that is formed for the final release of the Lord of the World to the devotees at the conclusion of a conference, you will know that all that I have told you is indeed true; and by the thread of contact with hierarchy which you have established, your life will never be the same.

Because of the increase of planetary levels of effluvia and of the descent of world karma in the Dark Cycle, our messenger has undertaken a program of weekend seminars scheduled between the quarterly conferences. These, too, are crystalline mandalas—jewels of perfection formed by the chelas working in consonance with the ascended masters.

Hierarchy bids you welcome into the flame of oneness where you will see and behold with the eyes of the soul how the messenger becomes the focal point for the offering of the energies of the group unto the hosts of the Lord and for the receiving of the word, the energy, the radiation, and the teaching of the Great White Brotherhood not only for those gathered but for all mankind, for all time and space. This is indeed the miracle of the age—the miracle of the transfer of cosmic energies and cosmic momentums through the power of the spoken Word.

Come and see. Come and see the place where the Word is made flesh[6] within you. Come and see the place where your soul, as a sphere of light, bounces on the trampoline of God's mind.

I look forward to greeting you personally through the messenger who focuses the feminine aspect of my being in form.

El Morya

CHAPTER 11

Chelas in Pursuit of the Light of Victory:

Victory is a light, a being, a consciousness. Victory is a flame whereby the collective will to failure focused in the subconscious of the race as a negative spiral of defeatism is inverted, overcome, and reestablished as the ascending cycle of the soul's reality. Victory is a magnetic momentum that builds the mountain of self which becomes the magic mountain of ascended being.

The laurel of my victory I place before the Christ Self of each one. And the will of El Morya, as the *energy-light* of the *Mo*ther *ray* within you, is the impetus that drives home by the action of the blue lightning of the mind of God the personal victory which you can and shall become.

I have watched the chelas who "know" the law. Yes, they can recite sacred Scripture; for as Jesus said, "In them ye think ye have eternal life: and they are they which testify of me."[1] There are those who always "know" the word. They quote the quotable quotes. They paraphrase the ascended masters. They are revered by other chelas on the path; yet in their lack of true understanding they lack the thrust of action, the will to be victorious, the love to be self-sacrificing. And so they cycle and recycle the ancient wisdom, going over and over the grooves of the memory of the laws of God, not knowing they are devoid of the spirit, the grace, and the fulfillment of the Lord of Being.

We come with the fire of God-victory that is a cosmic momentum of wisdom flanked by will-power and love-power. We come with a cosmic threefold flame to infuse knowledge with life, to confound the wisdom of this world that is foolishness with God,[2] to transform that wisdom by the power of his rod. We come to blaze the threefold action of the law that swirls as resurrection's fires through the brain, the mind, the consciousness, and the heart of chelas the world around who would, as one body, one flame, form the spire of victory.

We come in the name of the Christ. And in the flame of Jesus, by the authority of God, we exorcise the corridors of consciousness. We command in the name of the living God all discarnates, all fallen ones, and the splinters of divided unreality to come out from the temple of our God, to come out from the citadel of the chela's consciousness. We come to purge the cinders of the mind, the ashes of the burnt offering of selfhood. We come to sweep clean that place that is prepared to be the dwelling place of the Most High God, the individuality of man and woman.

Victory is the momentum of your ascension. Victory is the light of mercy whereby you forgive and forgive to the uttermost the soul's identification with the synthetic self. Without dalliance, without defense, the soul summoned by the Christ comes forth to make itself an acceptable offering unto the Spirit. As Saint Clare prepared herself to be the bride of the Perfect Bridegroom, so now let the soul, naked before God, be adorned as a bride prepared to meet her husband.[3] And let the golden light of victory converge in cosmic purity, veiled innocence, translucent face of Cosmic Virgin.

O chelas of the sacred fire, the winners are those who have the will to win! And the consciousness of failure is the consciousness of doom. Let it be shattered I say! And let it be cast into the sea! And the sea, as Mother flow, shall absorb mankind's collective will to failure. And as the light of victory streams through the bouncing surf, the tide of a Mother's love, fiery energy in motion, transmutes the fog of depression, the vanity of ego expression, and all not-self awareness outside the fiery core of our oneness.

Victory is the armies of the Lord marching toward the center, approaching the Arc de Triomphe in a radial pattern from the battlefields of life. And upon the tomb of the unknown soldier—the flame that marks the place where the lesser self has laid down its life for the Greater Self—let the testimony of the overcomers be written: "These are they who loved not their lives unto the death, chelas of the Word who overcame the accuser of the brethren by the blood of the Lamb and by the word of their testimony."[4]

Saint Francis was outspoken in defense of the Christ light. By espousing Mother Poverty, he made the impoverished self the backdrop for the appearance of the Christ in an age fattened by self-satisfactions, indulgence in carnal pleasure and carnal treasure. Will you do the same? Will you be the fiery cross of the converging of Father-Mother God? Will you place yourself at the nexus to be the witness of the bursting-forth of the light and the identity of the eternal Christos? "And the Word was made flesh and dwelt among us, and we beheld his glory, the glory as of the only begotten of the Father, full of grace and truth."[5]

Today the light must shine forth into the darkness of a world now bloated with the pollution of pride. The universal light streams forth. The light shines in the darkness and the darkness comprehends it not[6] until man and woman make personal that light by determining to be Christed ones. Then the personality of the Christ revealed as a living example will be understood and emulated. Come forth now, brave chelas! Show the biceps of warriors bold! Show your expertise in wielding the sword of living flame as you go forth to slay the dragon of the lesser self.

"And there was war in heaven: Michael and his angels fought against the dragon; and the dragon fought and his angels, and prevailed not; neither was their place found any more in heaven. And the great dragon was cast out, that old serpent called the Devil and Satan, which deceiveth the whole world: he was cast out into the earth, and his angels were cast out with him."[7] This record from the Book of Life is set forth in the revelation of Jesus Christ sent and signified by his angel to John the Beloved.[8] It is the record of the one who lost the victorious sense, lost the flame of victory, and fell into the vainglory of the pseudopersonality.

And the glamour of that synthetic self is the dragon's tail that drew the third part of the stars of heaven.[9] Thus the misqualification of the energies of the lower chakras and of the Mother flame, symbolized in the dragon's tail, caused many lesser angels to follow the one who was called Lucifer (light-bearer) together with his lieutenants, Satan, Belial, Beelzebub, Baal, and others. These demigods set themselves apart from the hosts of the Lord and the hierarchy of heaven. Having been cast out of heaven, they created their own kingdom of the underworld, commonly called the false hierarchy.

Once they were privileged to serve the living God as his emissaries. By their refusal to worship the image of God, the original matrix out of which the Lord God himself created the whole creation, including male and female as the positive and negative polarity of the Divine Whole, they were forced to descend into the planes of Mater. They lost their inheritance and their right to be joint heirs with Christ[10] until they should bow the knee and confess that the light which lighteth every man and woman[11] is not only the image of God but the God of all.

Therefore the warning went forth: "Woe to the inhabiters of the earth and of the sea! for the devil is come down unto you, having great wrath, because he knoweth that he hath but a short time."[12] Having been vanquished by Michael, Prince of the Archangels, these fallen ones became the prisoners of time and space, became corruptible and entered the spirals of disintegration and death. Since the fall of the Luciferians, the Satanists, and their cohorts, they have determined that as long as they were doomed to die, the children of God should die also. For the fallen ones have but one fear, and that is to die alone. Thus the archdeceivers of mankind, by their divide-and-conquer tactics, have devised all manner of witchcraft and black magic to torment the children of God and to draw their energies into alignment with their negative spirals, their defeatism, their despair, their despondency—their will to fail.

Now we look to the overcomers to challenge the enemy within and without, to expose the lie of the dark ones who seek to invade the mind and the emotions, creating moods and rationalizations. These archdeceivers of mankind continually masquerade as the true identity of the children of God. At every hand they seek to convince the chela on the path that his synthetic self is his Real Self.

I say to you now, your synthetic self is nothing but the fabrication of the collective consciousness of the fallen ones known as the carnal mind or the antichrist. All that seeks from within to condemn, to belittle, to downgrade, and to tear you from the love of God—this, precious ones, is but the movement of the downward spiral of those who dwell outside the kingdom—the consciousness—of our God. They have willed it so. Therefore, do not fall prey to their sympathies; for they would draw you into that spiral of self-destruction by the magnetic allure of their false personalities. They magnetize souls by the brilliance of their minds which they have stolen from the mind of God. Yet it is a perversion of that mind; it is the glitter of the carnal mind.

Beware the tinsel of their sharpened intellects. Beware the pull of their emotions. Beware the pride of the eye and of the evil eye and of a form and a countenance which, though simulating perfection, is hollow, vain, and without the quality of a humble humanity bearing the burden of the Lord's body. Beware the dragon that is wroth with the Woman, who goes forth to make war with the remnant of the seed of the Divine Mother.[13] For this one who employed the gift of free will to choose the not-self is indeed abroad in the planes of Mater, invading the etheric, mental, emotional, and physical bodies of the planet and its people.

These fallen ones continually present themselves as the saviours of mankind. These are the false prophets that come preaching the kingdom "lo here and lo there."[14] Believe them not. Follow them not, O chelas of the sacred fire. For the living God has placed his kingdom, as his consciousness, as his sacred fire, within you. Watch and wait for the fullness of the coming of the Lord as the law of your being, and do not accept the counterfeit creation. For they are the arch-enemies of mankind who are without scruples. These are the living dead who desire only one thing: to draw the living into their camp.

I AM the light of victory, and I AM the threefold flame of your Christ-awareness. I AM the champion of your overcoming. And by your word, which is the word of God, I stand in life this hour to challenge every challenger of the citadel of your God-reality, of your divine plan, and of the matrix of your soul. Call to me, and let us go forth arm in arm to join the hosts of the Lord. Look up and see the banner of mighty Victory and his legions. Look up and see how God is the defender of the light of victory within you.

Invictus, I AM the eternal flame that burns in the hearts of heroes and heroines of the ages!

El Morya

_____

CHAPTER 12

Chelas Who Would Become Defenders of the Faith:

And what of Michael, Prince of the Archangels, known as the Defender of the Faith? Micha-el! The name rings across the heavens like the resounding of the Liberty Bell. And the soul caught in the briars and brambles of astral configurations hears the cry of deliverance. Hail, Michael! Archangel of the Lord, radiantly arrayed in blue-white lightning and the yellow diamonds of illumined action that crown this son of light with victory.

The dawn cometh. And over the hills there can be seen in the early light the silhouettes of the hosts of the Lord. Legions of Archangel Michael, their shields reflecting a cross of white fire, their swords of living flame drawn in tribute to the Mother. Swords formed of the sacred Word which they intone, fired out of the vowels of their love for the living God. They are joined by the twelve legions of angels who gather at the command of the Faithful and True,[1] who also wield the sword of Christ, focus of faith, hope, and charity.

Chelas on the treadmill of life, yoked to the oxen of a mechanized Taurus substance by the lines of your own karma, look up! The deliverers of mankind are at hand. And Michael, Prince of the Archangels, leads the archangels and their legions in defense of the Christ consciousness. For God has ordained the evolution of the light through an infant humanity as that humanity reaches up to be the full expression of the seven rays of Christed awareness.

Chelas of the sacred fire, in this hour of compelling victory when victory's light surges from within and demands an outlet for the flow of love, I say respond to the call from within. Respond to the mandate of the inner law of your being to be the fullness of the Christ—God-victorious, love enthroned—crowning king and queen, while Father-Mother God ensconced in living flame cradle the Christ Child of their heart's oneness. And the fusion of that fire is for the mastery of the Christ consciousness in one of the seven rays. This day, I say, choose the path of your appointing and of your anointing. Apply to the inner law of your being and affirm God-reality as the cloven tongues of the Holy Spirit converge within you for the march to the summit of life's victory.

You have heard of the chohans of the rays. Now I say, invoke the momentum of the seven archangels to amplify in your soul and in your desiring to be whole the feelings of God which compel the entire consciousness into conformity with the geometry of selfhood. The seven archangels wield the power, the wisdom, and the love of Infinity—of a cosmos yet to be born within you as microcosmic-macrocosmic energies converge to become the warp and woof of the creative life force.

Now expand the cup of consciousness to contain the archangel of your ray. If you serve the will of God, then, on the blue ray, the first ray of the morning light, you define the azure of His Holiness. The one who stands before the altar of the Lord, the Adoring and the Adored, releases into the consciousness of the Archangel of the First Ray in sacred ritual a sphere of the will of God, a disc of flaming blue, a core of sapphire yod. Into his heart the great archangel absorbs an atom of energy, a globule of light. And rising from the altar of the Lord, he goes forth into the cosmos to release the cycles of God's faith—the will to be, the courage to live victoriously, the honor of the law, of life itself, and the energy to sustain a cosmic pulse.

In this blue fire flowing, received into the chalice of the Mother, is the blueprint of every form of life, the divine direction for fulfillment, the network of a cosmos and the egg and the I. And all the archangels and the seraphim and cherubim bow before the radiant wonder of the world— Archangel Michael, standing in the center of the sun, now become a sunlit sphere of blue, haloed with white-yellow brilliance as the diamond-shining mind of God exalts the warrior tried and true.

Chelas who would become aflame with faith, devotees of the will of God who would become more of self as the selfhood of his will, look up and behold the Captain of the Lord's Hosts—the great exemplar of your faith and your ray. And now, by invocation to your own I AM God Presence, submit by free-will edict of your soul all doubt and fear and every hesitation, all resistance to action that formulates the human question, and factors of disobedience to the word of the Logos. Submit them all to the conqueror. He, by the magnet of his love, takes into his heart fires, in response to the fiats of the chelas, all substance of negativity and the void of relativity.

As these energies cycle through the blue diamond on his heart's altar, the flaming sphere of blue is returned to you and you and you. This Archangel Michael has done as a mighty work of the Lord for peoples and nations and continents and worlds. Carrying the banner of the Cosmic Virgin, he stands; and he has stood down through the ages to defend the children of the Mother against the dragon Tiamat and her seed.

Now then, heed our call and heed his sacrifice. For this holy one of God stands before you. And as you read, each chela of the sacred fire receives the visitation of the Electronic Presence of Michael the Archangel. Won't you receive him in grace, in honor, and in thanksgiving? Won't you bid him enter the citadel of your being and offer unto him a cup of light, a cup of goodwill? While your Christ Self offers unto him the gifts of gold and frankincense and myrrh, let your soul not tarry in the shadows; but let it come forth and present also upon the altar of his flaming selfhood all hopelessness, faithlessness, acts of wanton selfishness, and every careless deed.

Allow the flaming one to assume the substance of your sin. Allow him to exchange it for the energies of his will to win. He will take unto himself that substance misqualified and transmute it into light, shining light—brilliant victory faceted in the mind of God. And so you lay the coals of a dying world of selfhood upon the altar of the archangel, and you watch as before your very eyes they are transformed into the diamond of your crystallized Christ-identity. This is the alchemy of the first ray. This is the movement of a mighty ocean that is the power of the will of God to suddenly be still. . .and become the drop of individuality.

I shall return to pursue our course of meditation in the mantle of the seven archangels who even now are knocking at the door of consciousness.

Morya

_____

Chelas Who Would Run to Greet
the Morning Light of the Archangels:

Each of the seven archangels carries a sphere of the
energies of God, a portion of the ray on which he serves.
Each day in sacred ritual, kneeling before the altar of the
Lord in the Great Central Sun, he receives his sphere and
he is commissioned to go forth throughout the cosmos to
scatter the seeds of Christic light that burst from the ray and
the sphere of the ray which he bears within his heart as a
great sun disc of emerging Christ-identity.

And the twin flames of the archangels and their legions
which comprise the hosts of the Lord Christ bow also before
the sons and daughters of God, acknowledging the sacred
fire upon the altar of the heart. Each day the sons and
daughters of God evolving in Mater have the opportunity to
receive the energies of one of the seven rays cycling from
the sphere of light held in the heart of an archangel.

Thus Michael, Jophiel, Chamuel, Gabriel, Raphael,
Uriel, and Zadkiel[1] place before the sons and daughters of
God the Electronic Presence of that selfhood which is one
in God, their own self-realized awareness of God in the first

;econd ray of wisdom, the third ray of love,
purity, the fifth ray of truth, the sixth ray
: seventh ray of freedom. For this reason
th among the early Christians, "Be not for-
␀␀␀␀␀ ␀␀␀␀␀␀␀ strangers: for thereby some have enter-
tained angels unawares."[2]

Receive the Lord's appointed spirits with the salutation
"Hail, flaming one of God! Welcome, son of the Most High!
Enter, thou servant of the Lord, Come into the sanctuary of
being where the kingdom of God is come into manifestation
on earth as it is in heaven." For thereby you open the valve,
as it were, at the nexus of the figure eight and the energy of
the great sphere does flow, cycling from the planes of Spirit
into the planes of Mater. And in your adoration, your willingness to be the instrument of the Lord's host, you give the
response of Mary to Gabriel the Archangel, "Behold the
handmaid of the Lord; be it unto me according to thy
word."[3] And your response is also a sun of reality, a sun of
light, a sphere of energy rotating within your heart.

And thus by the spherical momentum of your own devotion that rises over the same figure-eight pattern, connect-
ing your soul to the Spirit of the archangel, the cycling and
recycling of energies "as above, so below" is given added
impetus. And as the energies of the servant of God flow
into your being, your energies of aspiration, inspiration, of
striving to be whole, ascend to the heart of the archangel.

This is your daily offering. This is plugging into the
Source of infinity and using the symbol of infinity, the
figure-eight spiral (seeing yourself as the lower sphere and
the archangel as the upper sphere), as a visualization and an
actualization of that which is taking place. Here and now cosmic forces coursing—coursing through cosmic arteries—
conduct the currents that are for the sustainment of the

heart, the mind, the body, and the soul of God in Mater as in Spirit.

As Jophiel comes with golden sphere of glowing yellow fire and you receive unto yourself this hierarch of wisdom's flame, not failing to proclaim the personification of the law, unwilling to bypass hierarchy, there is imparted unto you the golden liquid light, nourishment for mind and nerves, stimulus for the crown chakra of Buddhic enlightenment. And you are aware of who I am and that I AM WHO I AM.[4] Self-consciousness. Awareness. Affirmation of being. "I think, therefore I am."[5]

Knowledge of selfhood comes with the flow of wisdom's fire. And as your four lower bodies are filled with the knowledge of the glory of the Lord as the waters cover the sea,[6] so you know that in the understanding of the law is the reward of your faithfulness and your courage to be and to live in obedience to the will of God. And in the joy of wisdom's glow, the soul lifts up a voice of gladness: "I will sing of mercy and judgment: unto thee, O Lord, will I sing. I will behave myself wisely in a perfect way. O when wilt thou come unto me? I will walk within my house with a perfect heart.[7] I will live in the joy of a present knowledge of the Lord and my heart will sing unto thee all the day, for I am awakened unto life and consciousness. Because thou art, O God, I am."

Now cometh the archangel of love, sphere of brooding tenderness haloed by fire of Holy Spirit—roseate quartz, a crystalled form, repository of pink infired love divine. I greet thee, O lord of love, Chamuel, flaming one. I am become a son of righteousness by love and the movement of love in my very soul. In the alchemy of the third ray, all human sorrow and sin is washed away.

In the flame of responsibility I respond to my ability to be like him. And in the likeness of the image of love, I am

one with every part of the Great Whole. And in that oneness there is born the perfect Christed Self of all. And by
loving the likeness of the one, I am become that likeness.
Sculpted by the hand of the Master, I am formed and re-
formed until my soul awakes in the likeness of the living God.

In love I am satisfied, fulfilled; for I have entered the bliss
of the eternal reunion with my Maker. I thank thee, O archangel of love, for passing through me, for allowing me to
pass through thee. And in the exchange of spirals of identity, I am become thy awareness of cosmic love; and all lesser
awareness is consumed by thy heart burning with love for the
eternal God and his creation locked in Matter-form and
formlessness.

Hearken unto Gabriel, Archangel of the Annunciation,
who cometh to announce the virgin birth of thy soul. O
Lord, I am made whole! As thy white-fire sphere of Alpha-
to-Omega enters my being, lo I am one with the Great Central Sun, a magnet of self-awareness as the Beginning and
the Ending[8] fills my soaring sense and I hear the call of the
Lord's Spirit "Arise, and take the young child and his mother,
and flee into Egypt, and be thou there until I bring thee
word: for Herod will seek the young child to destroy him."[9]

Thus the Angel Gabriel brings the warning of the Lord
unto all who would bring forth out of the white-fire core the
action of the Mother flame and the Christ Child of a selfhood immaculately conceived. Seal thy energies in the white
sun, in the heart of Mother Earth, symbolized as the land of
Egypt nourished by the Mother-flow of the Nile. Seal the
Mother and the child in the white chakra "until the death
of Herod"[10]—until the death of the carnal mind and of the
Antichrist who sends forth the hordes of night to slay all of
the children that are in Bethlehem, the place where God is
consecrated as the Word made flesh.

As the milk of the Word fills my cup, I grow and wax strong in the Lord. I increase in wisdom and stature and I find favor with God and man.[11] I am filled with the Holy Ghost. I am born of the Cosmic Virgin. I accept the benediction of my God "Thou art my beloved Son, in whom I AM well pleased."[12] Being filled with the Spirit of the living God, I am willing to be disciplined in the law and to receive the testings of the tempter,[13] that I might prove the wholeness which I am.

Now cometh Raphael, and the sphere of cosmic abundance is transferred to me. In the flow of emerald crystal fire, I perceive the true science of being—the science of the Christ whereby I prove true Christianity and the way of Buddha as one flame. I see the procession of healing angels— the Order of the Emerald Cross—carrying a banner now unfurled of pure white embroidered with sacred motif—an emerald cross entwined with pink rosebuds in remembrance of the blossoming of Aaron's rod,[14] a cross crowned with the crown of life, golden, fired out of the many crowns of this world laid at the feet of the King of Kings and Lord of Lords.

In awe of truth I meditate before the archangel whose soul sings, "Ave, Ave Maria." I merge with Raphael's devotion to the Mother crystallized in Mater as the pyramid of life, the City Foursquare,[15] and the Mater-realization of Spirit through science and the law of the abundant life. How bountiful are thy blessings, O God! Deal bountifully with thy servant, that I may live and keep thy word. Open thou mine eyes, that I may behold wondrous things out of thy law. . . . And I will delight myself in thy commandments, which I have loved. My hands also will I lift up unto thy commandments, which I have loved; and I will meditate in thy statutes.[16]

> Precipitation is the law of Mother-flow
> Coalescing molecules of Spirit here below.
> Where'er the grace of Mother's mind
> Is received with graciousness in kind,
> Chelas of the sacred fire will find
> Abundant measure, Mater-creativity consigned.

Enter Uriel, lullaby of love flowing as selfless service, purple and gold sphere, alchemy of self-transformation. I am become the servant of all. I live to serve, I serve to live. My life I give; and in the allness of my gift, I become the allness of his life. With mercy and compassion I move with the Prince of Peace bestowing the kingdom of heaven to the poor in spirit, comforting those that mourn, blessing the meek with their rightful inheritance, filling those who hunger and thirst after righteousness, extending mercy to the merciful, revealing God to the pure in heart, calling the peacemakers to be the children of God, imparting the kingdom to all who are persecuted for righteousness' sake.[17] I rejoice and I am glad in the light of ministration. For as I anoint the body of the Lord, I behold the Christ, I am that Christ reborn.

Come, O Zadkiel, in freedom's joy! Come in mercy and justice true. Come with sphere of violet hue. Come, O come! Bless me through and through. For I would be the ritual of the law that is the transmutation of every flaw of consciousness and character. I watch now as the Archangel of Aquarius pours the liquid fires of freedom as the universal solvent of all sin and sordid selfishness. I am washed clean by the water of the Word. My soul is free to be and to live in eternity. My soul is free to be the fullness of the law of the seven rays.

I would enter the priesthood of Melchizedek.[18] I would finish the course that I have set with the sealing action of the seventh ray and the ritual of the Logos he does outplay through the many actors on the stage of life. Electrodes are they! Of that Life particular and universal! They tend the fires of the archangels; they keep the flame of the chohans. As stars fixed in the firmament of God's being, these actors play their roles. And the role is a giant scroll on which is written the law of life for each personal personality of the sons and daughters of God who will to be the Christ and through the Christ become emissaries of the Holy Spirit.

This is the way of the seven rays with the seven archangels. Let your meditation be upon the spheres of consciousness of God's own Self-awareness, and let that awareness merge with the sphere of selfhood that you are. Go forth, then, to defend the faith, the hope, the charity in every aspect of the law, in every facet of the seven rays. Be champions of the light even as your victory is championed by the archangels of the Flaming One.

I AM the guardian of the soul's devotion to the will of God,

CHAPTER 14

Chelas Who Would Keep the Flame of Life:

"Hold fast what thou hast received!" is the fiat of the Lord pronounced by his hosts as they pass the torch of life to every Keeper of the Flame. Like the runners of ancient Greece who waited to seize the torch from the previous runner in the race, chelas of the sacred fire figure in the plan of hierarchy as they take up the torch of the Holy Spirit and of the Maha Chohan,[1] the Keeper of the Flame of Life.

All who would count themselves as members of the Great White Brotherhood must understand the responsibility of hierarchy. The torch is indeed passed to a new generation of lightbearers. The torch must be accepted gladly by an outstretched hand, a strong arm, a pure heart, and a mind holding God-control over the four lower bodies. The torch must be carried joyfully in the race of life and then graciously passed by the mature to the youth waiting on the line for those who have given their all and received in return the all of the Lord.

Hierarchy is composed of runners in the race. Hierarchy is a cloud of witnesses witnessing unto the truth of the ages. Hierarchy is keepers of the flame of life passing the torch of the Holy Spirit to all generations. "Wherefore," as it is written, "seeing we also are compassed about with so great a cloud of witnesses, let us lay aside every weight [of karma] and the sin [the sense of struggle] which doth so easily beset us, and let us run with patience the race that is set before us."[2]

Like Jesus, in whom we find the beginning and the ending of the cycles of Alpha and Omega converged in his great example of the Christ consciousness, like him whom we exalt as "the author and finisher of our faith" because he contained the "body" and the "blood" of the eternal Christos, like him we endure the cross, we prepare for the initiation of the crucifixion, for the joy that is set before us. And by God's grace, when we shall have run the race we shall also be "set down at the right hand of the throne of God."[3]

In January 1961 I authorized the formation of the Keepers of the Flame Fraternity to be formed of a circle of devotees within The Summit Lighthouse who would give supreme allegiance to the flame of life and to the Knight Commander, Saint Germain. I invited all who would pledge their support to this hierarch of the Aquarian age to participate in a worldwide endeavor to draw into the flame of the Holy Spirit sons and daughters of God who would come forward to claim their inheritance as joint heirs of the Christ consciousness.[4] And so the call went forth to all who had stood before the Lords of Karma at the Court of Justice vowing to implement the plan of hierarchy for world freedom. These are they whose souls, as they descended into embodiment, uttered the fiat of the messengers of the Lord, "Lo, I AM come to do thy will, O God!"[5]

Just as unascended chelas of the law have obligations to hierarchy, a responsibility to mankind, and a duty that is their dharma to fulfill the inner law of their being, so

ascended hierarchs have their obligations to those above
and below them in the scale of hierarchy, not the least of
these being to their unascended chelas. Therefore, in order
to provide opportunity for service to all, to meet the requirements of the law "as above so below," and to release a gnosis of ascended-master law into hands outstretched and
hearts uplifted, Saint Germain went before the Lords of
Karma once again. He asked for and received the dispensation to place his purple cape, the mantle of his service,
upon the altar of humanity, and specifically upon the altar
of all true devotees of the flame of freedom—those destined
to be the avant-garde of the Aquarian age.

To those who would give their support shoulder to
shoulder to the ascended masters and to our messengers
Mark and Elizabeth Prophet for the promulgation of au-
thentic teaching delivered unto them by the hierarchy, a
special invitation was extended by the Knight Commander
and me to affirm their sponsorship and their commitment
by joining this outer fraternity of the Great White Brotherhood. To all who would recognize the Prophets as they serve
in the office of the two witnesses prophesied in the eleventh
chapter of the Book of Revelation, to all who would understand the need to keep the flame of life on behalf of a humanity unenlightened and unawakened in memory of the
Ancient of Days,[6] the invitation was given.

Those who responded are those who understood from
deep within the soul the need to reconsecrate that flame
through daily invocations and decrees made in the name of
the I AM Presence and the Christed Self of all mankind—
those who were eager to pursue the alchemy of the Spirit
and to work directly with Saint Germain to precipitate the
foundations of the golden age. Those who have remained
constant to their pledge have also understood the need to

sponsor the teachings through regular financial support of our organization, The Summit Lighthouse. And over the years they have affirmed their loyalty and their oneness, their willingness to sacrifice, if necessary, lesser causes and concerns for the greater cause of the Brotherhood on earth, the cause to which their souls were already dedicated in heaven.

Wherever the ascended masters have worked diligently to establish a focus of their teaching, there has always been an attempt by the dark ones to usurp the authority of the prophet, the teacher, or the messenger through control of the purse strings. This occurred in the early formation of The Summit Lighthouse. At that time the messenger totally rejected both the purse and the person of one whose financial backing, offered in exchange for the control of our organization, could have brought him world renown. It is often the case in this world that those who control the supply also control the policy of institutions public and private.

Thus in those early days when the very fate of a planet seemed to hang in the balance as a few chelas made their decision, some questionable and questioning and some quick to leap as a flame in the service of Saint Germain, the Knight Commander exclaimed: "O for ten thousand scrub-women who will faithfully give to the cause! With these I will show you how to change the world with divine truth."[7] Therefore a nominal initiation fee and monthly dues were set to offset the control of the few by the support of the many.

Chelas of the sacred fire who would become alchemists of the Spirit must understand the requirements of the law. Whereas we send forth the teacher and the teaching, those evolving in the planes of Mater must demonstrate their devotion to both teacher and teaching by demonstrating through the laws of alchemy the precipitation, whether directly or indirectly, of the necessary supply for the expansion of the work and the multiplication of our word throughout the body of God. Ours is the descending triangle of the Logos, and yours is the ascending pyramid of the mastery of the material plane.

By the law of alchemy, as you give regular support—heart, head, and hand—to our cause through the Keepers of the Flame Fraternity, we are authorized to deliver into your hands instruction in cosmic law that has already laid the foundation for the ascension of not one but a number of Keepers of the Flame. These have both received and applied the monthly lessons written by the hierarchy, presenting step by step the certain knowledge of the law that leads each Keeper of the Flame on the path of initiation to the door of the I AM Presence who declares, "Behold, I AM the open door which no man can shut!"[8] Here at the feet of the chela's own living masterful Presence of Life, the torch that he carries in his right hand bursts into the ascension flame and he is received from the sight of mortals into the cloud of sacred fire[9] with which his soul merges at the conclusion of the race.

The Keepers of the Flame Fraternity is a universal spiritual order dedicated to eternal faith, unwavering constancy, and infinite harmony with the love of God that is forever the radiant flame called life. Keepers of the Flame live for the flame of life, and Keepers of the Flame are the lively stones in the temple of our God.[10] They uphold the flame of life as the threefold flame ablaze within their hearts, a focus of overcoming victory to negate personal and planetary spirals of death, disintegration, and decay. The flame of life which they keep within their hearts is a sacred fire blazing higher and higher as they invoke the action of the seven rays of the

Christ consciousness. Thus the white fire, in answer to the call of each Keeper of the Flame, takes on the hues of the seven rays as they apply to the flame of God-mastery under each of the chohans of the rays.

Keepers of the Flame are responsible to the spiritual board of the fraternity, which is headed by the Maha Chohan, the Keeper of the Flame, and the Knight Commander, Saint Germain. The board of directors is composed of the seven chohans, who direct various aspects of the unfoldment of the law both through the printed instruction and through the individual training which Keepers of the Flame are given in the etheric retreats of the Great White Brotherhood. A special Committee for Child Guidance formed for the preparation of parents of incoming souls and for the proper education of children is headed by the World Teachers, Jesus and Kuthumi, together with Mother Mary. All who uphold the honor of the Keepers of the Flame and live according to the principles and precepts of the law find an acceleration of both inner and outer discipline which comes to them out of the living fount of joy and gratitude which the hierarchies of heaven hold for all upon earth who are willing to give a more than ordinary support to the cause that is paramount to the salvation (self-elevation) of humanity.

Upon the founding of the fraternity, the spiritual board, with the assistance of the entire Great White Brotherhood, ordained and dedicated the Keepers of the Flame Lessons as an official channel which should serve to further enlighten mankind and to vanquish ignorance by the light and power of the God flame. And it was determined at the Darjeeling Council table that the sacred knowledge of the flame which the masters are pledged to release in these lessons should provide a safe platform for ascending souls—a path so well lighted that none who examine the teachings and

pursue them with an objective heart should ever hesitate to
cross the threshold into eternal life and the truth that shall
make all mankind free.[11]

Those who have faithfully served the cause of the Brotherhood through their support of the Keepers of the Flame
Fraternity have been amply rewarded with countless blessings. One and all, though sometimes unbeknownst to their
outer consciousness, have had the opportunity to attend
closed classes in the retreats of the masters, as well as at our
quarterly conferences, and to balance an extraordinary
amount of karma through their application to the violet
flame multiplied by the sponsors of the fraternity (the members of the spiritual board), who enter into a direct and inti-
mate relationship with each chela who is willing to make
the commitment that is required.

Make no mistake. Though organizations have failed,
though individuals have betrayed the trust of God and man,
the Great White Brotherhood continues to sponsor qualified
leadership in outer activities and to use them both as the
threshingfloor where the chaff and the wheat may be separated to prove who is worthy of association with hierarchy.
The Keepers of the Flame Fraternity and The Summit
Lighthouse are such organizations, and our messengers are
examples of individuals sponsored by hierarchy to represent the true Church Universal and Triumphant to all who
are able to receive them.

The fact that some have failed does not mean that all will
fail, for I am here to tell you that in the cosmos the victories
far exceed the failures. And thus we are gurus in search of
chelas who are willing to give that total support to the flame
of God-reality which is the foundation of every victory. As
Saint Germain set forth the requirements of the hour as
constancy, harmony, and loyalty, so I add to that list courage,

ingenuity, and a daring to love God and his anointed servants all the way.

Some of you are aware of the fact that I was embodied as Arthur, king of the Britons, and that I shared with Launcelot and Guenevere the dream of the Knights of the Round Table and the quest for the Holy Grail. Some of you know that Merlin, the court magician, was a living embodiment of Saint Germain, who held the flame of prophet, counselor, and alchemist during my reign. Now let it be known that Camelot was a dream of the lowering from the etheric plane into the physical, as one of the Father's many mansions,[12] of a nucleus of lightbearers, representatives of the twelve tribes of Israel and the true Israelites whose pledge is also to the Christ and to the flame of reality in all that *is real.*

And let it be known that the messenger Mark was my chela in Launcelot and that my beloved Queen Guenevere was his twin flame, your own Elizabeth whose Mother's heart now belongs to the world. Let it be known that that triangle of mutual love which we shared focused the Trinity of Father, Son, and Bride of Holy Spirit and that the oneness which we pledged and our devotion to the crystal light and the goblet of our Lord is renewed each day as we partake, as above so below, of the communion cup of life. And the three dots which are the Mark of Morya in devotion to the Mother are the sign of our thrust for a purpose and of Camelot come again.

The Keepers of the Flame Fraternity is presently composed of souls who have been with us through the ages as we have sought and found the Holy Grail. And one by one, those who have made themselves worthy have also found their places reserved at the round tables of the etheric retreats of the Brotherhood. In this fraternity sponsored by our Merlin, we work hand in hand to realize the dream that was so long ago, the dream that is reborn within our hearts as a matrix of victory in every age. Thus in the ceremonies of the Keepers of the Flame meetings, there is the opportunity for initiates of an extraordinary devotion to be knighted by the Knight Commander and to be sealed as ladies of the flame. Others who have embodied a certain virtue with steadfastness, in patience waiting upon the Lord,[13] may be given the title of brother or sister of the flame.

Chelas who remember the flame at Camelot, chelas who understand the need to maintain the thread of contact with hierarchy and the continuity of the unfoldment of the plan century by century, will run with the call of Camelot and the response that only love can give, "To you I give my all!"

Keepers of the Flame, onward in the search for the Holy Grail! With the banner of the World Mother, the heart of the Knight Invincible, the shield of Archangel Michael, and the sword Excalibur, we shall not fail!

I AM Arthur in the mantle of

Morya

*Chelas Who Would Replace the Love of the
Lesser Self with the Love of the Greater Self:*

There is a story in Greek legend about a beautiful youth who gazed into his reflection in a pool and fell in love with the image. As he pined away in the love of the lesser self, he was transformed into a narcissus and to this day is remembered by that name.

And so as you look at the daffodils and narcissus, yellow and gold in the springtime breezes, moving gently in the fresh winds of Aries and Thor, remember the devotion to the lesser self that, through the alchemy of the Holy Spirit, became in the floral offering the devotion to the Greater Self.

Sometimes mankind who abuse the gift of free will find that in the mercy of the law their energies, cycling through nature, are balanced through the elemental kingdom as plant and animal life take on the burden of mankind's karma. Thus through the fires of transmutation and through the sacrifice of the lesser evolution for the greater, all life evolves Godward toward the center of the Divine Ego which ultimately displaces all egocentrism in the understanding of the adoration of the self as the great God Self.

The worship of the lesser self is illegitimate. The worship of the Greater Self is legitimate. Therefore in the evolution of mankind, those who have allowed themselves to become attached to the form and the form consciousness have always found that their love is linear, following the finite line that has a beginning and an ending. By and by these learn the lesson that every ascended master has learned, that love is spherical and that true love is a whirling sun within the heart.

Ignited by the Holy Spirit, its devotion is to the flame of life in every self, in every part of the Great Whole. And through devotion to the flame, the spherical love of the Greater Self takes in, in expanding measure, the allness of the lesser self, including its form and its formlessness, so that true love, all-encompassing, includes the Whole and the part.

True love meets the human need as well as the divine. True love can be experienced only as the completeness of the Higher Self is reflected in the pool of the soul. Thus beholding the Great Spirit, the great reality of selfhood, man and woman fall in love with the image of God and are consumed thereby. And in the consuming is the consummation of a greater love than any which can be contained in the cup of consciousness here below. Yet that greater love, shared by the Father-Mother God with every son and daughter, includes the allness of creation, the vastness of a cosmos.

In the relationships of God with God as these are experienced in life on earth, God gives to mankind a sip of the communion cup of love which only he can give. He allows him to partake of that immortal love which, through the fusion of the lesser self with the Greater Self—of the soul with the Spirit—all shall one day share as the joy of the rapture, being caught up in the resurrection fires of the Christed ones.[1]

Hierarchy comes to shorten the days of tribulation[2] for all who have caught the vision of the goal. Straight as the arrow flies, so is the soul shot from the bow of the Eternal Archer. Passing through the planes of Mater with the momentum and the thrust of the great arm of life, the soul reaches the mark of love and transcends all lesser images of selfhood. The arrow hits the zero in the center of being— zero ego, zero self-awareness apart from God. Here individuality is forever defined as an arrow aflame, so pining for the Real Image as to become a magnet magnetizing the energies of the Great Central Sun, including every virtue and talent that counts in the expansion of selfhood in and as the Holy Spirit.

Hierarchy comes to save the devotees from the shipwreck of a mortal existence confined and confining to mortality, possessed by and possessing lesser selves, forms of idolatry and of the idolatrous generation. Hierarchy comes with a call to the disciples of Christ who would become fishers of men. Hierarchy knows who and where you are. As Jesus walked by the Sea of Galilee and marked Simon and Andrew, already marked by the inner law of being, as they cast their net into the sea and said unto them, "Come ye after me, and I will make you to become fishers of men,"[3] so the call goes forth from the hierarch of the Aquarian age to disciples of the Flaming One of Freedom.

And those who have the marking of the law upon their souls will, like them, straightway forsake their nets and follow him, leaving friend and foe alike to follow the one through whose great heart fires all mankind shall be drawn into the net of the Cosmic Christ consciousness. And so the "fishes" merge into the oneness of the Greater Self, into that love which is above all other loves even as the *loaves* were also formed of the love of the Father-Mother God. And their allegiance is that which commands the very electrons of the soul as it gazes into the pool of the Self to form the image of its Maker.

The mark of the fish taken by the early Christians is not only the mark of the Piscean conqueror who conquers the emotions of a planet by the water of the Word, but it is the sign of those who have made the twin arcs of Alpha and Omega coils in the caduceus of the divine polarity. And the dot of the eye is the point of infinity where you are.

To souls adrift upon the sea of life we send out a line. It is a lifeline that must be seized with trust; for without trust, the doubts and fears of the lesser self, with all of its anxiety and frustration, inundate the soul that pursues the reunion with the Spirit of the living God. In taking up the line, the chela makes a choice. It is a choice to be led, that it might one day lead. And there is a daily choice also: to hold on to the line or to let go.

The ascended masters do not force their chelas. They allow their chelas to force them—to magnetize them—and thereby magnetize themselves to the higher law of their own being. There is a certain friction that is required for all attainment on the path. There are inconveniences to be borne and perhaps incongruities as you find yourself at times out of alignment with the lever of the law. Chelas must be willing to exert themselves. Exertion is the block and tackle of mind and soul lifting the weight of darkness that it might become light. And there is a staying power that must needs be tested, a hanging-on for life, for breath, for love, for wholeness.

We write our *Pearls of Wisdom* out of engrams of light, out of matrices of the Spirit. Paragraph by paragraph, the sacred formula of selfhood unfolds. Man must decipher the formula of life and of living. He must probe. He must read and reread. He must invoke the Holy Spirit in whose flame is to be found the interpretation of the living Word and the multiplication of the loaves and fishes, numbers of the law that are imparted as the equation of Spirit and Matter both between and in the lines of the printed word.

We will not spoon-feed our chelas. We expect to be met at least halfway. The oatmeal is on the spoon. Let those who are hungry lean forward, take the spoon, and feed themselves! We demand the mind of the chela conform to the mind of God. Hence our method in the presentation of the law is often after the koan of the Zen masters. We allow the enigma of divine reason to challenge human reason, to force the soul to a new plane, the plane of the rationale of the eternal Logos.

Our courses of instruction are not presented as a one-two-three, do-it-yourself success formula. We are not interested in "making business" or in popularity with the mass consciousness; nor do we play up to the sick and dying ego grasping and gasping in the throes of a final thrust for recognition through the emotional or mental control of other egos. We do not promise to do for our chelas what they must do for themselves. Such systems involving the manipulation of aspects of the self appearing here and there as courses in auto-hypnosis, mind control, and the mechanical "clearing" of subconscious patterns or the records of past karma are but psychic hooks that have snared the souls of thousands. One and all these are but the *manipollution,* as the Great Divine Director says, of those who are on an "ego trip" outside the living flame. Let them have their day—for the days of their ambition are numbered.

Ah yes, our writings contain the sacred formula; but for the formula to crystallize in the mind of the chela, there is a requirement. That requirement is the input of the chela—

the soul ingredient. The chela must mix in the momentum of his own individualized God flame. Our discourses are distillations of the Spirit. Like the many instant foods on the shelves of your supermarkets, our words are concentrates: you must take them home and add water. The water is the living Word that flows freely from the fount of the Divine Mother. By God you are the Word incarnate! Shall we then add insult to injury by adding the water for you? Bah! Morya says, mix your own brew!

By the alchemy of the master and the chela, by the fusion of selfhood as above so below, there emerge from the printed page and from the spoken Word a definition of concepts and the sacred formula that is unique for each individual even while it affirms the universal law of the elements. This interaction takes place each time the chela brings the flow of selfhood, of experience gained as it moves through time and space, to the instruction of the ascended masters.

Thus the association of the chela with the master is unique in each and every case. For every lifestream there is a special oneness all its own, and each encounter is a special moment in eternity when time is not and space is consumed. These experiences with the ascended masters come day by day to those who will to leave behind the patterns of the lesser self and merge with the solar consciousness of the Greater Self as they study the *Pearls of Wisdom* and the Keepers of the Flame Lessons and meditate upon the dictations of the hierarchy delivered through our messengers Mark and Elizabeth Prophet.

Now and then we hear the outcry of the proud intellect who takes up a *Pearl of Wisdom* and then declares, out of the ego need to impress his peers or to intellectually justify his rebellion, "I don't get anything out of the *Pearls*." Well, poor moth, I say, what do you expect? After all, you put nothing into them. Each *Pearl of Wisdom* is a key to another facet of the master's consciousness. And if, like the moth, you dare approach the light without your own light, you will, like the moth, be consumed.

If you love the master, you will infuse the *Pearl* with your own momentum of devotion to the law and to the teaching. And this, together with the worded release, will unlock the light of the causal body of the teacher. Some will try to take the teaching without giving of themselves. These retain a mental awareness and a mental attitude. They are devoid of the Spirit; their cups are empty. Having received nothing, they have nothing to give.

The same law holds true as you read the sacred scriptures of the world, for the true masters of the ages have never cast their pearls carelessly.[4] They have revealed part of the mystery through the spoken Word and part through the unspoken word of their example. Beyond that they have let the inner law of each one's own being act to compel the soul to rise to the level of the Christ consciousness. Here, received by the individual I AM Presence, it receives the gifts of the Spirit locked in the worded matrix now unlocked by the I AM THAT I AM. "For we know in part, and we prophesy in part. But when that which is perfect is come, then that which is in part shall be done away."[5]

Let all then accept the challenge of finding the pearl of great price[6] locked in each *Pearl of Wisdom*. Let them think twice before casting aside that which to their outer sophistication seems overly simple or overly complicated, too shallow or too deep, behind the times or ahead of the times, as the case may be. Let them think twice before casting aside the opportunity to come into union with the Spirit of the living God.

Humanity are all divers diving into the great sea of life.

ʰat if the pearl diver dives into the ocean it is not the fault of the ocean. Oppor-ﾉands in the hourglass eternally flowing through ﹍ and space. Opportunity is to seize the grain of the moment and make it a living pearl. Opportunity is to take the pearl of self, of a soul translucent, reflecting rainbow hue of Elohim, and to cast it into the sea of life that others might find in the pearl of selfless selfhood the way that leads to an eternal individuality.

In this age the ascended masters have cast the pearl of their identity sealed in God into the great sea of humanity in order that humanity might find their own individuality and their soul similarly consigned to God.

I AM the pearl waiting for the diver. Come and find me.

El Morya

The El of the Mother Ray
in the Eye of the Flaming Yod

_____

CHAPTER 16

Chelas Advancing in the Art of Communication:

The Word is all and everything. The Word is the eternal Logos. It is the voice of the Ancient of Days thundering the Ten Commandments from Horeb's height, etching out of the living flame the markings of the law on tablets of stone. The Word is the will of the AUM and the ray of your divinity. The Word is life and love and truth. The Word is law and principle. The Word is individuality through and through.

We send forth messengers of the Word whose souls, anointed by God himself, have knelt before the altar at the Court of the Sacred Fire and received the commission of the Four and Twenty Elders.[1] And their authority is that of the Great Central Sun messengers. To be a messenger for hierarchy is a high and holy calling—one that is not lightly given, one that ought not to be lightly received.

Down through the centuries we have appointed our messengers, prophets of the law, teachers of the way of the Christ consciousness and of the Buddhic light. Others whom we would call unappointed, or self-appointed, messengers have come forth to blatantly usurp their ministry and their office in hierarchy. And so there is abroad in the land an enticing spirit, beguiling as the serpent, that is not the true spirit of prophecy. Nor is it come as the gift of the Holy Spirit;[2] it is the voice of rebellion and of witchcraft, of vain talkers and deceivers.[3] These are the crystal-ball gazers, the psychic readers and self-proclaimed messiahs—bewitched and bewitching, coming in the name of the Church yet denying the true Church, coming in the name of the Logos yet their lives a betrayal of true reason and the law.

They are the archdeceivers of mankind. They would take over the person and the personality of the ascended masters and the real gurus. Setting themselves up as gurus, they sit in the lotus posture smoking the peace pipe with the false hierarchy, dispensing drugs along with demons, and even training their disciples in the manipulation of sexual energies for heightened sensual gratification. In their all-consuming lust for power, they teach the way to God through sexual perversion, abuses of the body, and the desecration of the Mother. And the light they steal from those they ensnare is used to satisfy their mad cravings and to control vast segments of the population through witchcraft, variance, and mortal cursings.

Others are in the business of training "channels" and psychic healers. They know not the difference between spiritual and psychic energies—the pure and the impure stream. Thus the gullible they make channels for the energies of the pit, for the diabolical murmurings of familiar spirits and of "wizards that peep and that mutter."[4] The false hierarchies and the fallen ones come in many guises, seeking to impress an infant humanity with their sleight of hand, trance and telepathy, their flying saucers and other trappings.

I say woe to those who are adept in the mental manipulations of Matter and astral energies yet have not the Christ—the snake charmers and charlatans who display a phenomenal control of bodily functions yet have not one iota of soul mastery! As if they had a thing to offer mankind which mankind cannot get directly from their own Christ Self, their own I AM Presence, and the living flame which God has anchored within the heart!

Some of these, deceived and deceiving others, go so far as to say that everyone should be a psychic channel, everyone should develop his psychic powers. Like the magicians in Pharaoh's court,[5] they hold up to our messengers their psychic phenomena and they say, "See, we do the same thing!" Not so! Like the fallen ones who, in their attempt to level hierarchy, would make themselves equal with the sons and daughters of God, these psychic channels would cause our messengers and their work with the living Word to become muddied by the flood of psychic material being released by the false hierarchy.

Let it be so! They have free will. As the grass of the field, they have their day; for the wind passeth over them and they are gone, to be remembered no more.[6] But the day of the true messengers of hierarchy shall be as the giant redwood marking the cycles of the spiritual-material evolution of the race and as the snow-covered Himalayas outlining the pinnacles of soul attainment. Thus the prophets have come in every age, and their day is the day of the salvation (self-elevation) of the race of mankind. And the coming of the messenger is always the preparing of the way for the coming of a new level of the Christ consciousness. "Behold, I send my messenger before thy face, which shall prepare thy way before thee."[7]

In every century the messengers have proclaimed the living truth that should free mankind from age-worn doctrine and dogma. In this age they have come to prepare the world to receive their own Christ-identity and the I AM Presence "coming in the clouds of heaven with power and great glory."[8] Their coming marks the hour when all who have realized the oneness of the I AM Presence through the ritual of the ascension should appear to mankind through the exalted vision of the Christ consciousness. Not only Jesus, but Mary, Saint Germain, Gautama Buddha, Confucius, Mohammed, and all who have attained oneness with the eternal flame of life through the ritual of the ascension— these shall appear to mankind in the Second Coming once mankind themselves have accepted the law of the I AM Presence and their own identity as Christed ones.

The true messengers of God receive only the word of the Great White Brotherhood and of the ascended masters. Their communion is not with the dead, nor do they practice necromancy or spiritism or hypnotism or the mesmerism of the mass consciousness. They are forbidden by cosmic law to allow their chakras to be instruments for the fallen ones, to channel the energies of disembodied souls abiding in the astral realm, or to be the mouthpiece of discarnates or any of the rebellious spirits which comprise the false hierarchy.

This is the age of the testing of the spirits. Therefore, as John said, "Try the spirits whether they are of God."[9] How does one try the spirits? Blessed ones, you challenge every voice within or without which comes to you in the name of the Lord:

"In the name of the living God, my own I AM Presence, and by the flame of Jesus the Christ, I challenge every voice that speaks from within or from without. And I say, I demand that you show forth your light! I call forth the flame of the Holy Spirit to consume in you all that is less than God's perfection. I call forth the Elohim and the all-seeing eye of God to expose the truth, to expose the lie, and to strip all mortal consciousness of its mortality. Let it be replaced here and now with the immortal flame of God-reality.

"In the name of the Christ, I call to the Elohim Astrea to encircle the cause and core of every spirit of deception, self-deceived and deceiving. I call to Archangel Michael to cut me free by the action of the sword of blue lightning from every entity inhabiting the astral plane, from all denizens of the deep. And I call to Mother Mary and her virgin consciousness to intercede for me in the name of Jesus the Christ, that my soul and my four lower bodies might be preserved as a chalice of purity to receive only the word of Almighty God and his true emissaries. So let it be done in the name of the I AM THAT I AM! And let the hosts of the Lord come forth to defend the Word incarnate in the souls of all mankind."

Precious ones moving toward the center of the I AM THAT I AM, the ascended masters and representatives of the Great White Brotherhood, whether on this or any system of worlds, will never be offended by this invocation. Those who are offended, both giving and taking offense, are not of the Christ. Every emissary of the light is required by law to show forth the credentials of his light to all who demand those credentials. Therefore, speak with the voice of one who has the authority of the Christ and the commandment of God; and accept the covenant of Jesus given unto his disciples "Verily, verily, I say unto you, Whatsoever ye shall ask the Father in my name, he will give it you. Hitherto have ye asked nothing in my name: ask, and ye shall receive, that your joy may be full."[10]

It is lawful to question the purveyors of the false teachings and those whose lives do not bear the fruits of living truth. As it is written, "By their fruits ye shall know them."[11] And so without hesitation Jesus cursed the barren fig tree, saying, "Let no fruit grow on thee henceforward for ever";[12]

for the elemental spirit thereof had failed to provide fruit for the souls of mankind. Thus is the judgment of the Four and Twenty Elders pronounced upon those false hierarchs of the age even as Jesus spoke unto those who proclaimed themselves authorities of the law: "Woe unto you, lawyers! for ye have taken away the key of knowledge: ye entered not in yourselves, and them that were entering in ye hindered."[13]

Let it be known, then, that sweet water and bitter do not come forth from the same fount.[14] Likewise, those who have failed to surrender the lesser self unto God, those who have failed to make this sacrifice, are not counted among our emissaries. They come teaching in their own name instead of in the name of the ascended masters. Instead of giving God the glory, they pursue the vainglory of name and fame for their teaching or their system or their methodology. These are they who come preaching the kingdom, saying, "Lo here!" or "Lo there!" who fail to acknowledge that the kingdom of God is within you.[15] They make themselves gods before men. Being themselves idolaters of the lesser self, they receive the idolatry of the lesser selves of their followers while failing to exalt the Higher Self.

And so as the messenger of Jesus instructed John the Revelator who fell down to worship him, "See thou do it not. . .worship God,"[16] and as the commandment was given, "Thou shalt have no other gods before me,"[17] so we say, worship God as the I AM THAT I AM. With all thy heart, with all thy soul, with all thy mind, worship him.[18] For the act of worship is an action of flow. It is a flow of energy from your soul that makes an arc with the object of your worship. It is the energy of devotion. And therefore if the object of your devotion be any aspect of the lesser self, God's energy in you flows to that self, forming the arc of idolatry. And one day the idol will come crashing down, broken before your feet;

and it will be the arc of your own energy that destroys both the idol and the idolater.

The testing of the messengers is the testing of the decibels and of the cycling of the energies of infinity through form and consciousness. Where there is light uncontaminated by the darkness of ego and ego manipulation, where there is a dazzling sun of glory and real contact with hierarchy through the power of the spoken Word, where there is the conveyance of the Christ mind, there stands the messenger of the Great White Brotherhood.

And so the messenger of the covenant shall suddenly come to his temple.[19] His temple is the heart of man. He is the Christed one standing at the altar of the sacred fire to read the proclamation of deliverance—the deliverance of the soul into the arms of Almighty God. And so the Christed one releases the statement of the law even as that statement has been sent forth by the messengers whom we have chosen and ordained.

In 1876, Helena Petrovna Blavatsky was ordered by the Master Kuthumi and me, then known as the Masters K.H. and M., to write *Isis Unveiled.* Later she was given the responsibility of imparting *The Secret Doctrine* to the world. Commissioned by Jesus the Christ, the Ascended Master Hilarion, and Mother Mary, Mary Baker Eddy was given certain revelations which she set forth in *Science and Health with Key to the Scriptures.* Though at times beset with their own preconceptions and the burden of the mass consciousness, these witnesses codified the truth and the law of East and West as the culmination of thousands of years of their souls' distillations of the Spirit.

Such messengers are not trained in a day or a year or a lifetime. Embodiment after embodiment, they sit at the feet of the masters and receive the emanations of their mantle in the power of their word and example. A number of others who were selected to perform a similar service for hierarchy failed in their initiations through the pride of the intellect and their unwillingness to submit identity totally unto the flame. They have become thereby totally self-deluded and they continue to draw innocent souls into the chaos of their delusion.

In the 1930s came the twin flames Guy W. Ballard and Edna Ballard imparting the sacred mystery of the law of the I AM, further knowledge of hierarchy, the invocation of the sacred fire, and the path of the ascension. Representatives tried and true of Saint Germain, they were commissioned to remain the only messengers of the hierarchy of the Aquarian age until mankind should redeem a certain portion of their karma.

When that cycle was fulfilled, Saint Germain, together with the Darjeeling Council, sponsored Mark and Elizabeth Prophet to carry on the work not only of the Ballards and the I AM movement, but also of Nicholas and Helena Roerich. The Roerichs set forth the word of Morya destined to reach both the Russian and the American people with the energy and the enlightenment that should deter the red dragon[20] of World Communism. And so the Mother flame of Russia and the Mother flame of America converge in spirals of freedom and victory for the sons and daughters of God in both nations and in every nation upon earth.

Hierarchy is no respecter of persons, of politics, or of polemics. Hierarchy's call knows no barrier. It cannot be stayed by the iron curtain or by the iron wall that a mechanistic civilization has erected around the children of God. The beam of our eye is a laser beam; it is the action of the ruby ray. It goes straight to the heart of the devotee; and no hand and no force and no ideology can stay the will of the master who sends forth that ray to call the souls of God home. Let those who reckon otherwise beware. For I have spoken; and the Lord has said, "So shall my word be that goeth forth out of my mouth: it shall not return unto me void, but it shall accomplish that which I please, and it shall prosper in the thing whereto I sent it."[21]

I conclude my letters to chelas on the path with the exhortation of the apostle of the early Church whose office is now filled by the Mother of the Flame: "Feed the flock of God which is among you, taking the oversight thereof, not by constraint, but willingly; not for filthy lucre, but of a ready mind; neither as being lords over God's heritage, but being ensamples to the flock. And when the chief Shepherd shall appear, ye shall receive a crown of glory that fadeth not away."[22]

When Peter was confronted with the ultimate test of sacrifice, he attempted to remove himself from the fiery core of the Christ, from the center of the flame and of the Mother. Fleeing Rome to escape martyrdom, he met the Lord Christ along the Appian Way and asked his master, "Quō vādis?— Where are you going, Lord?" Jesus answered, "I go to Rome to be crucified again." And so Peter accepted his destiny, turned in the way, went back to Rome, and was crucified for his Lord.

To all who are confronted with the temptation to withdraw from the Christ, from the Mother, or from the path of initiation, I say, go back! Go to Rome—there to be crucified for your Lord, there to lay down the lesser self, that the Christ may appear not only in you, but in the hearts of all mankind.

And the promise of the Second Coming is fulfilled each time you lay down the life of the lesser self that the Christ might take it again and go forth to work his works through you as apostles of the Church Universal and Triumphant, as disciples of Christ, as ministers and teachers, healers and counselors, as servants, scientists, artists, and artisans of Spirit and Matter.

Go forth in the name of God and in the name of Jesus the Christ. Swiftly, fearlessly, run to greet your divine destiny there at the nexus of the fiery cross where God and man meet in a conflagration of the Holy Spirit that is the essence of living love.

I AM Morya waiting for the knock of the chela at the door of the Darjeeling retreat.

ABRAHAM, Hebrew patriarch and progenitor of the twelve tribes of Israel (c. 2000 B.C.). Jews, Christians and Moslems accord him the place in history as the first to worship the one true God. In the biblical account of his life, he is originally referred to as Abram (meaning the father, or my father, is exalted). God later named him Abraham, which is traditionally taken to mean "father of a multitude of nations" but is currently thought by scholars to be a dialectic variant of Abram.

Scholars once widely assumed that Abraham was either a mythical being or a simple nomadic or semi-nomadic Semite. They claimed that the biblical narrative of his life could not be read strictly as a biography because it was written more than one thousand years after the events it described. As Richard N. Ostling wrote in *Time* magazine, many liberal Bible scholars treated Abraham "not as a historical figure, but as a sort of Semitic King Arthur." Recent finds, however, have forced scholars to reevaluate the traditional image of the patriarch. Since World War I, archaeological finds at two third-millennium B.C. cities, Ebla and Mari, have revealed that a sophisticated literary and urban culture existed before and during Abraham's time.

The Bible first depicts Abraham and his family as citizens of Ur of the Chaldees—the flourishing cultural, political and economic center of the technically advanced Sumerian civilization. Sir Leonard Woolley, head of a British-American team of archaeologists that excavated Ur shortly after World War I, wrote, "We must revise considerably our ideas of the Hebrew patriarch when we learn that his earlier years were spent in such sophisticated surroundings; he was the citizen of a great city and inherited the traditions of an ancient and highly organized civilization." The first-century Jewish historian Josephus indicates that Abraham was a man of noble birth and military might. Eminent biblical archaeologist William F. Albright advanced the theory that Abraham lived around 1800 B.C. and "was a wealthy caravaneer and merchant whose relations with the native princes and communities were fixed by contracts and treaties (covenants)." Others have described the patriarch as the charismatic chief of a clan of herdsmen, farmers and warriors.

Scholar Zecharia Sitchin claims that Abraham was a Sumerian nobleman born as early as 2123 B.C. who was descended from a priestly family of royal blood and who had a large household and a private army. The Book of Genesis, in fact, portrays Abraham as a "mighty prince" in the land—a powerful chieftain who deals with kings, makes military alliances and negotiates land purchases. He loves peace, is skilled in war and magnanimous in victory. He embodies the ideals of justice, righteousness, integrity and hospitality. He is also described as a prophet and an intercessor before God. But, most important, Abraham is the prototype of the man who holds strong to his faith in the LORD's repeated promises that he will be a "father of many nations," even when outer circumstances seem to indicate just the opposite.

Genesis tells us that Abraham, his father and his family left Ur to dwell some 600 miles away in Haran, a major commercial center in northwest Mesopotamia in the Fertile Crescent (where Syria now is). Although the Bible is silent on Abraham's early years, Jewish oral tradition says he was engaged in a battle to win converts to monotheism. He is said to have smashed the idols of his father, Terah, an idol maker, who the Book of Joshua says "served other gods."

The Bible records that when Abraham was 75 and his father had died, the LORD called him to forsake all—his kindred and his father's house, the culture and cults of Mesopotamia—and journey to "a land that I will show thee." The LORD promised: "I will make of thee a great nation." Abraham left Haran with his wife, Sarai (whose name was later changed by God to Sarah), his nephew Lot, and "all their substance that they had gathered and the souls that they had gotten in Haran." When they arrived in the land of Canaan, the LORD appeared to Abraham and promised, "Unto thy seed will I give this land."

When a severe famine struck the land, Abraham traveled south to Egypt. Afraid that the Egyptians would kill him because his wife was such a beautiful woman, Abraham represented Sarah as his sister and allowed the Pharaoh to take her into his household. As a result, the LORD plagued the Pharaoh and his house. When the Egyptian ruler learned the truth, he quickly sent Abraham and Sarah away with all the servants, cattle and riches Abraham had acquired in Egypt.

Once back in Canaan, the herdsmen of Lot and Abraham began to quarrel and the two kinsmen separated. Abraham generously offered first choice of the territory to Lot. Lot settled in the fertile plain of Jordan toward Sodom while Abraham dwelt in the seemingly less desirable land of Canaan in Hebron. After Lot departed, the LORD told Abraham that he would give to him and his seed all the land that he could see—north, south, east and west. And although the patriarch was still childless, the LORD affirmed that his seed would be as innumerable as "the dust of the earth."

Next, the Bible depicts Abraham as a military leader. When a powerful coalition of kings captured Lot and all his possessions, Abraham armed 318 of his own "trained servants" and joined other chieftains in the land to defeat them and save Lot. Returning from this victory, Abraham was blessed by Melchizedek, king of Salem and priest of the most high God (El Elyon). Melchizedek "brought forth bread and wine" and Abraham gave him a tithe (tenth) of the spoils. Abraham then returned all the captives and goods that had been plundered to the king of Sodom and refused the king's offer to partake of the goods himself.

The Bible also depicts Abraham in the role of intercessor. The LORD confided to Abraham his intention to destroy the wicked cities of Sodom and Gomorrah. Abraham secured God's assurance that Sodom would be spared if but ten righteous men could be found therein. Although the city was ultimately destroyed, two angels warned Lot of the impending calamity and he escaped.

Despite the LORD's repeated promises that Abraham's seed would become innumerable, Sarah was still barren after ten years in Canaan. She proposed, after the custom of the day, that

Abraham sire a child by her maid Hagar. Hagar then bore
Abraham a son, Ishmael. Thirteen years later, when Abraham
was 99 and Sarah 90, the LORD revealed himself to the patriarch
as El Shaddai, "the Almighty God." The LORD established an
everlasting covenant with Abraham to be a God unto him and
his seed. He revealed that Sarah would bear a son, Isaac, "at this
set time in the next year" and that Isaac, not Ishmael, was to be
Abraham's heir. As the LORD had prophesied, Sarah finally
"conceived and bare Abraham a son in his old age."

Yet the supreme test of the patriarch's faith was still to
come. God commanded him to sacrifice his only son and long-
awaited heir upon a mountain in the land of Moriah. At the
end of a three days' journey, Abraham built an altar, laid Isaac
upon the wood, and raised his knife to slay the young boy when
the angel of the LORD called out, "Lay not thine hand upon the
lad, neither do thou any thing unto him: for now I know that
thou fearest God, seeing thou hast not withheld thy son, thine
only son from me." Abraham sacrificed a ram instead, and for
the final time the LORD confirmed his covenant with Abraham.
After Sarah passed on, Abraham married Keturah, who bore
him six children. Although the patriarch provided for his other
children, he "gave all that he had unto Isaac." Abraham died at
the age of 175 and was buried beside Sarah in the cave of
Machpelah, which is hallowed today by Jews, Christians and
Moslems—all of whom trace their origins back to Abraham.

Abraham's personal relationship with God and his exem-
plary faith have earned him the title "Friend of God" in both
Christian and Moslem scriptures ("El Khalil" in the Arabic lan-
guage of the Koran). He is, as the apostle Paul says in Romans,
the father not only of the Jews, but "of all them that believe."
The Moslems (who believe that the Arabs are descended from
Abraham through Ishmael) revere the patriarch more than any
other figure in the Bible. Inscribed on the Jaffa Gate in the Old
City of Jerusalem is the passage from the Koran, "There is no
God but Allah, and Abraham is beloved of Him."

MELCHIOR, one of the three wise men who paid homage to
the Christ Child. Adoring the will of God in the radiance of the

Son of God, it was Melchior who perfected the science of heavenly bodies and the cycles of cosmic astrology. He followed with mathematical precision the star of the Presence of the Manchild born to the Virgin Mary, and he carried the precious gift of gold—the golden electrode of the Mind of God, that mind which was to be perfectly manifest in the universal consciousness of Christ Jesus; the gold of the King of Kings, the Prince of Peace; the gold of the teaching of the eternal Christos, the Son, that steps forth from the golden Sun of Righteousness; gold—the abundant life that he would restore to all, the offering of his Mother to her children.

In a dictation given April 16, 1976, El Morya described the experiences of several of his soul's early incarnations, perhaps on Mercury, which prepared him for his embodiment as Melchior: "How many aeons ago did I become a chela of the will of God before I even knew the meaning of the word *chela* or of the concept of the Guru? But God to me was the golden light of the dawn. And I sensed in the first rays of the dawn the will of a cosmic purpose—the will of a Life and of a Creator beyond myself. And for a number of incarnations the focal point of my observation of the Deity was the morning light of the sun. And by and by through that contact, unbeknownst to me, with Helios and Vesta, there was established an arc—an arc of flow over the arc of my own attention. And I began to feel the response of my own God flame within to the God of very gods in that Sun behind the sun.

"The observation of this attunement with Life continued for several more embodiments until I was not able to even begin a day of my life without this contact and this flow of energy—a literal infusion of my consciousness with ideas, with the understanding of the work that I should do. Almost, as it were, at subconscious levels I would move into and out of the sun as my point of contact. And so it came to pass as my devotions increased and the concentration of energies increased within my chakras, that after succeeding embodiments I contacted a teacher—a teacher of the ancient science of astrology. It was the science of the study of heavenly bodies and their influences upon the evolutions in time and space. And that teacher gave me insight into the energy and the contact that I had made with the very core of creation. And so it was by will, not my own yet which I made my own, that the contact with Life was established, that it grew and expanded. And the light of Helios and Vesta that glowed within my heart became a magnet—a magnet of the pursuit of God through the application of science.

"I have always, then, followed the path of science, whether on Mercury or on Earth or other planetary homes of this system and other systems of worlds. The LORD God has permitted me to understand the law of the heavenly bodies and the earthly bodies and of the flow of energies in time and space. And I have found myself becoming one with the cycles of Matter for the mastery of those cycles, almost, as it were, going within within the heart of Matter before going to the outside of Matter. Growing from within—from within the sun within the earth and the Sun behind the sun—I learned the way of God and God's laws by the inner geometry of the molecule, the atom, the Cosmos. And my appreciation of that which I did not at first call God came through the humble awareness, the awesome awareness of this thing—this thing that is Life, this thing that is energy, this thing which is the harmony, this thing that I now behold as the will of God."

ARTHUR, KING OF ENGLAND. Into the midst of a war-torn and superstitious people Arthur came as a mighty conqueror. Indeed, the Arthurian age is the starting point of British history. Upon his tomb in the cathedral at Glastonbury the epitaph reads: "Hic jacet Arthurus rex quandam rexque futurus"— Here lies Arthur, the king that was and the king to be.

The exact dates of the life of Arthur are unknown, although his story is recorded in both history and legend throughout western Europe. He first appeared in the sixth century when King Uther Pendragon died without an heir to the throne. The vicious power struggle which ensued could only be resolved by Merlin, the alchemist. In the churchyard of the Cathedral of London he caused the miraculous appearance of a large, foursquare stone with a steel anvil upon it and a sword thrust into the anvil. On the stone, the inscription: "Whosoever pulleth this sword from this stone and anvil is rightwise born king of all England."

The trial of the sword represents the power of the soul that is free from the bondage of attachment to things material, symbolized by the stone and anvil. It is an illustration of the divine right of kings—he who has the greatest attainment of the Christ consciousness has the right to rule. Knights and warriors, kings and noblemen gathered from throughout the western world, but Arthur alone, a lad of twelve, could free the sacred sword. He was crowned King of England by the Bishop of Canterbury.

At Camelot, King Arthur called together men and women of the highest attainment from throughout the realm and formed the Order of the Knights of the Round Table. Their raison d'être: the quest for the Holy Grail, the defense of the Mother principle, eternal brotherhood under the Eternal Father, the restoration of Christ's kingdom on earth, the protection of the flame of the Holy Spirit in the community of Arthur's court and its extension throughout Britain, and the ennoblement of the soul through devotion to the Christ in individualized community action. The knights of the Round Table and the ladies of the court at Camelot were initiates of a mystery school of the Great White Brotherhood. In the tradition of the Pythagorean school at Crotona, the Essene community at Qumran, the mandala of Christ and his apostles, as well as the guilds of medieval Europe that would succeed them, the knights and ladies guarded the inner truths of the Brotherhood revealed to them by Saint Germain, who was embodied as the beloved Merlin, the court magician and counselor to the king. The jousting and competition of the knights in their tournaments was the measuring of levels of inner soul attainment.

The devotion of King Arthur and Queen Guenevere in their soul relationship of guru and chela was the focus of the flame of the Father-Mother God in the center of the court. The coming of Launcelot du Lac, also a chela of Arthur, to the Order of the Knights of the Round Table was the drawing together of the three persons of the Trinity, the threefold flame in the heart of Camelot. The soul relationship of

Launcelot and Guenevere was that of twin flames. Together Arthur, Guenevere, and Launcelot laid the foundation of the Christian/Piscean dispensation for the English-speaking peoples.

Arthur beckoned his knights to quest the Holy Grail, the cup from which Jesus drank at the Last Supper. According to legend, the Grail cup was deposited in a well at Glastonbury by a group of disciples who, together with Mary the Mother and Joseph of Arimathea, journeyed by boat from the Holy Land to establish shrines on the European continent and in the British Isles for the expansion of western Christendom during the next two-thousand-year cycle. Thus El Morya, anointed by God (through Merlin, the reincarnated Prophet Samuel, anointer of kings and prophets unto the people Israel), attuned with the Grail focus and by his noble ideals and spiritual genius, built the platform for the dissemination of the Christic light throughout the globe wherever the British went forth by its impetus to discover and settle new worlds. The inner significance of the knight initiates of the brotherhood of the quest was seeking and finding the Christ consciousness through the law of self-disciplined service to life.

Among the knights of the Round Table, Sir Modred (said to have been Arthur's son sired prior to his marriage) harbored intense jealousy and hatred for the king. Knowing that the military strength of Arthur was unsurpassed, he contacted the sorceress, Morgana le Fay, and together Modred and Morgana used the subtle entrapments of witchcraft, treachery, and intrigue to destroy the sacred trust of king, queen, and knights of the Round Table. In a war that resulted from the denial of a Roman demand for tribute, Arthur would have conquered Rome itself and the entire empire if he had not been called back to England where Modred had usurped the throne and imprisoned Queen Guenevere in the Tower of London. In the fierce Battle of Camlam that followed, Arthur slew Modred but was mortally wounded. It is said that as Arthur lay dying on the battlefield, he sighted a young boy and in him beheld the hope of the future. The king knighted the lad and bequeathed to him the precious vision of Camelot come again. Then, as the story goes, Arthur was placed on a barge with three mysterious queens and taken to the island-valley of Avalon, as Tennyson wrote,

> Where falls not hail, or rain, or any snow,
> Nor ever wind blows loudly; but it lies
> Deep-meadow'd, happy, fair with orchard lawns
> And bowery hollows crown'd with summer sea,
> Where I will heal me of my grievous wound.

El Morya's dream to free the earth is far more than this brief span of knighthood. In this age, Arthur is ascended, holding the balance for his chelas, the twin flames Launcelot and Guenevere, reembodied as Mark and Elizabeth Prophet, whom he commissioned to reestablish the mystery school Camelot in that island-valley of Avalon—the Promised Land of the Woman clothed with the Sun (the Universal Mother) and the Divine Manchild she bears (the Christ consciousness quickened in the children of God on earth). On New Year's Eve, 1976, El Morya recalled the days of Camelot. He said: "Really, no time or space has passed in this joy of the return—all is as it was then, the return to the white flame, and before us the vision of the Grail that we must carry into the new world and into the new age."

THOMAS BECKET, Lord Chancellor of England in the twelfth century under Henry II. Thomas was a man of action, delighting in hard work and quick debate. As a young man, he was educated in the finest schools of Europe and served in the household of the Archbishop of Canterbury, Theobald, who introduced him to the king and recommended him for the chancellorship. Becket and the king were said to have been of one heart and one mind and it is likely that the chancellor's influence was largely responsible for many of the reforms in English law for which Henry is credited. Sir Thomas had a taste for magnificence and his household was considered even finer than the king's. Wearing armor like any other fighting man, he led assaults and engaged in hand-to-hand combat—strong willed, stern, yet blameless in character and deeply religious.

In 1161, Archbishop Theobald died and Henry called Becket

to fill the office. The chancellor declined, however, warning the king that such a position would separate them on moral principles. Sir Thomas told him: "There are several things you do now in prejudice of the rights of the Church which make me fear you would require of me what I could not agree to." The king paid no heed and hastened to have Thomas consecrated archbishop on the octave of Pentecost, 1162. Obedient to the king and in loving submission to the will of God, Becket left his household and his finery and began the life of an ascetic. Next to his skin he secretly wore a hairshirt. The beloved archbishop spent his days distributing alms to the poor, studying holy scripture, visiting the infirmary, and supervising monks in their work. Serving as an ecclesiastical judge, Thomas was rigorously just.

Although as archbishop Becket had resigned the chancellorship against the king's wish, nevertheless, as he had foretold, the relationship between Church and State soon became the crux of serious disagreements. Since at that time the Church owned large parcels of land, when Henry ordered that property taxes be paid directly to his own exchequer—actually a flagrant form of graft—Thomas protested. In another matter, a cleric accused of murdering a king's soldier was, according to a long-established law, tried in ecclesiastical court and was there acquitted. A controversy arose because Henry considered the archbishop a partial judge. The king remained angry and dissatisfied with Thomas and called together a council at Westminster where the bishops, under pressure from the king, reluctantly agreed to the revolutionary Constitutions of Clarendon, which provided certain royal "customs" in Church matters and prohibited prelates from leaving the kingdom without royal permission. These provisions were severely damaging to the authority and prestige of the Church.

Heedless of the new law, Thomas crossed the Channel to put the case before the Pope. Bent on vengeance, the king commanded him to hand over certain properties and honors and began a campaign to discredit and persecute him. King Louis of France was inclined in the Church's favor and accepted the archbishop in exile. While submitting himself to the strict Cistercian rule in the monastery at Pontigny, Thomas received a letter from the bishops and other clergy of England deploring his "hostile attitude" to the king and imploring him to be more conciliatory and forgiving. Becket replied: "For a long time I have been silent, waiting if perchance the Lord would inspire you to pluck up your strength again; if perchance one, at least, of you all would arise and take his stand as a wall to defend the house of Israel, would put on at least the appearance of entering the battle against those who never cease daily to attack the army of the Lord. I have waited; not one has arisen. I have endured; not one has taken a stand. I have been silent; not one has spoken. I have dissimulated; not one has fought even in appearance. . . . Let us then, all together, make haste to act so that God's wrath descend not on us as on negligent and idle shepherds, that we be not counted dumb dogs, too feeble to bark."

The historic quarrel had dragged on for three years when at last King Louis was able to effect a partial reconciliation between Thomas and Henry. But when the archbishop returned to London on December 1, 1170, he was met with fierce hostility. Three bishops who had been excommunicated by Thomas for direct disobedience to the Pope went before Henry, who remained yet in France. In a fit of anger, Henry shouted words which four of his knights took as cause to set out for England, to arrest the archbishop while he was in the sanctuary of Canterbury Cathedral, and there to insult and brutally murder him. The incredible sacrilege of murdering an archbishop in his own cathedral produced a reaction of horror throughout Christendom. When the news was brought to the king, he realized that his mistaken remark had caused Becket's death. Henry shut himself up and fasted for forty days and later did public penance in Canterbury Cathedral.

The body of Thomas Becket was placed in a tomb in the cathedral, which became the focus for hundreds of thousands of pilgrims—immortalized by Chaucer in his *Canterbury Tales* —who came to the shrine, where many reported that miracles were wrought by Becket's intercession. Within three years, Thomas Becket was canonized a saint and martyr. The motion picture *Becket,* based on the play *Becket* by Jean Anouilh, is the dramatic portrayal of the life of Thomas Becket.

SIR THOMAS MORE, celebrated today as "a man for all seasons," was born in 1478 in the heart of London. His father, a prominent lawyer and judge, provided him with an excellent education. At eighteen, he left Oxford with a thorough knowledge of the classics and devoted himself to the study of law. Young Thomas was already a close friend of the eminent Dutch humanist Erasmus and was growing in favor with King Henry VIII, who employed him in missions abroad. Also pursuing his literary interests, More was acclaimed as the first writer of elegance in English prose for his *Life of Richard III,* a precise historical document which Shakespeare followed in literal detail.

More's deep devotion to God caused him at one time to consider a religious vocation and to practice extraordinary austerities for over four years to test his own self-discipline. He decided to marry, however, and his wife and four children proved to be his greatest joy and his sole comfort in days to come. Their famed estate at Chelsea housed Thomas' entire family, including eleven grandchildren. Over the years, More's "little Utopia," as he often called it, became a center of learning and culture, likened by Erasmus to "Plato's academie"—a home of good will to which came the most learned men of the day, even the king himself, for counsel and for comfort. At Chelsea, More wrote the famous work entitled *Utopia,* a witty exposé of the superficiality of English life and the imperfections of English law.

In 1529, Sir Thomas More was appointed by Henry VIII Lord Chancellor of England. Of him Erasmus wrote: "In serious matters no man's advice is more prized, while if the king wishes to recreate himself, no man's conversation is gayer. Often there are deep and intricate matters that demand a grave and prudent judge. More unravels them in such a way that he satisfies both sides." In spite of many honors and achievements, More sought no man's esteem. He remained sensitive to the needs of the common people by daily walking the back streets of London to inquire into the lives of the poor. And even as Lord Chancellor, it was his daily custom to enter the court of judges at Westminster Hall where his father sat, to kneel, and to ask his blessing.

Sir Thomas devoted himself to his duties with utmost zeal until Henry, desirous of but lacking a male heir to the throne, declared his marriage to Catherine of Aragon null and announced his intent to marry Ann Boleyn. Since the divorce was without papal approval and directly opposed to the laws of the Church, More refused to support the king's decision. He resigned his office and retired to Chelsea, where, greatly concerned with the heresies of Luther's revolt, he continued his writings in defense of the Catholic faith. Without friends and without office, More and his family lived in abject poverty. Nevertheless, Henry had been insulted at the chancellor's public disapproval of him. The king, therefore, sought to defame More and thus restore his royal image.

When Sir Thomas clearly refused to give the oath of supremacy to Henry as head of the new Church of England, he was imprisoned in the dread Tower of London. Badgered by the king's lawyers, More staunchly refused to compromise the position of the Church but diplomatically avoided direct accusation of the king, thereby saving his life and remaining a testimony to Henry's sinful injustice. Finally, however, jealous enemies were encouraged by Henry to lie against him in the chancellor's own court at Westminster. Charged and convicted of high treason, Thomas More was beheaded on Tower Hill in 1535. Kneeling before the executioner, he said, "I die the king's loyal subject but God's first." Sir Thomas More was canonized a saint in 1935. The motion picture based on the play by Robert Bolt, *A Man For All Seasons,* is the story of the life of Sir Thomas More.

AKBAR THE GREAT. When Akbar Jalal Ud-din Mohammed inherited the throne in 1556, the sixteenth-century Mogul empire of India had been effectively reduced by fierce alien conquest until only the capital city, Delhi, remained. Not yet fourteen at his accession, the brilliant young emperor set out to reconquer his realm. He became known throughout the world as Akbar the Great—the most powerful of the Mogul emperors.

Tremendous physical stamina characterized Akbar and contributed to his extraordinary military success. He could ride

240 miles in twenty-four hours to surprise and defeat the enemy. Nevertheless, it took the major part of his long reign (1556–1605) to subject the rebellious princes of northern India and to secure peace by establishing sound provincial governments. Akbar was endowed with a genius for administration. He increased trade efficiency by constructing roads, by developing advanced marketing systems, and by instituting postal services. In wise concern for all peoples under his jurisdiction, Akbar abolished the hated *jizya,* the poll-tax levied on non-Muslims, and gave Hindus prominent positions in government.

The new capital city, Fatehpur Sikri, soon became a flourishing cultural center larger than the city of London at that time. There Akbar assembled scholars of the Muslim and Hindu sects, Jains, Zoroastrians, and Jesuits. He later built an *ibadat khana,* a "house of worship," where learned men of all religions could meet to discuss both theology and philosophy. As a result, a new eclectic faith emerged called the Din-i-Illai (Divine Faith).

Akbar strongly supported Indian art, and under his direction more than one hundred workshops were established for the crafts. The emperor himself was very fond of music and encouraged it as a means of communication between Hindus and Muslims. Although illiterate, Akbar's library of illustrated manuscripts was as celebrated as the finest collections in Europe.

At the end of his reign, the peace and prosperity which Akbar had brought to India was disturbed by the court intrigues and subversive activities of his son, Jahangir. When he inherited the throne, Jahangir rejected his father's reforms, especially those of religious tolerance, and the empire rapidly crumbled. Jahangir's son, Shah Jahan, inherited only a small and unruly kingdom but retained a great love for the cultural heritage of his grandfather. As the greatest of the Mogul builders, Shah Jahan gave to India its most cherished monument: the Taj Mahal.

THOMAS MOORE, born in Dublin in 1779. A prolific writer of both prose and poetry, he graced the land of Erin with his tender love for God and man. He graduated from Trinity College in 1799 and moved to London. As an impressionable young man with a "quick Irish temper," the execution of a close college friend during the United Irishmen's Rebellion aroused in Moore a patriotic fervor that provided his greatest literary inspiration. His direct style and youthful attitude made him useful to the British liberalist cause as a witty satirist. His poems served as the controversial political cartoon of the day. Thomas Moore's greatest works included a brilliant biographical masterpiece taken from the confidential memoirs of Lord Byron. His own *Memoirs, Journal,* and *Correspondence* are an invaluable social record of life in England and Ireland during the first half of the nineteenth century.

Although he spent most of his life in England, Moore became known and loved as the national lyricist of Ireland through his *Irish Melodies*—a collection of verses written to the tunes of old Irish folk songs. The best remembered of these romantic ballads is "Believe Me, If All Those Endearing Young Charms," which to the present day draws the power of his intense love for the will of God.

> Believe me, if all those endearing young charms,
>   Which I gaze on so fondly to-day,
> Were to change by to-morrow, and fleet in my arms,
>   Like fairy-gifts, fading away,—
> Thou wouldst still be ador'd as this moment thou art,
>   Let thy loveliness fade as it will;
> And around the dear ruin each wish of my heart
>   Would entwine itself verdantly still!
>
> It is not while beauty and youth are thine own,
>   And thy cheeks unprofan'd by a tear,
> That the fervour and faith of a soul can be known,
>   To which time will but make thee more dear!
> No, the heart that has truly lov'd never forgets,
>   But as truly loves on to the close,
> As the sun-flower turns on her god, when he sets,
>   The same look which she turn'd when he rose.

ASCENDED MASTER EL MORYA. Describing the ultimate victory of his ascension and his work with mankind from the ascended state in the dictation given April 16, 1976, the master said: "Through countless incarnations and services rendered to the hierarchy, learning the ways of the world and the ways of the cosmos, I came to the place where I could follow the ray of my own God Presence back to the heart of the Flaming One. And so at the conclusion of the last century, I followed that ray to the white-fire core and I did not return with the dawn of the morning light to Mater, but I accepted the ritual of the ascension for one purpose: to serve the will of God in a greater capacity than I was able while in embodiment."

El Morya ascended in 1898 following his work with the Master K.H. in founding the Theosophical Society. Today, Ascended Master El Morya holds the office of Chohan (Lord) of the First Ray of God's Will. He represents the Godly attributes of courage, certainty, power, forthrightness, self-reliance, dependability, faith, and initiative. These are the qualities of the Father principle—the statesman, the executive, the ruler. Because he has ably outpictured these essential virtues, El Morya has, through many embodiments, worn the crown of authority, ruling many kingdoms wisely and well. His rulership has not been that of a dictator, demanding that his subjects submit to his human will. Rather, his interpretation of government is "God-over-men" and his concept of true statesmen is "God's overmen." He inspires illumined obedience to the holy will of God.

El Morya is the hierarch of the Temple of Good Will in the etheric plane over the city of Darjeeling, India, in the foothills of the Himalayas. This retreat is a mandala and a forcefield that is used by the solar hierarchies to release increments of cosmic energy to the planet. Together with the members of the Darjeeling Council and the Brothers of the Diamond Heart who serve at the Darjeeling retreat, El Morya assists mankind by organizing, developing, directing, and implementing the will of God as the foundation for all successful organized movements.

El Morya says, "My service then continues from the Darjeeling Retreat of the Brotherhood where I am counseling, with other brothers of the will of God, so many of the evolutions of earth who serve in the governments of the nations, who serve as teachers and scientists and musicians, and those who control the flow of the will of God that is power, that is the abundance of supply. The will of God is applied in all levels of human endeavor, for the will of God is the blueprint of every project. It is the foundation of every task. It is the skeleton of your body. It is physical energy. It is etheric fire. The will of God is the fiery diamond in your heart."

The diamond-shining mind of God is the very heart of any endeavor. Public servants, world and community leaders, and holders of public office are schooled between embodiments and in their finer bodies during sleep to renew the charge of Morya's thrust for a purpose and to refresh their understanding of the intricacies of the will of God in politics, in religion, in business, and in education. Ascended and unascended masters and their chelas meet at Morya's retreat frequently to discuss national and international problems and the means to their solution. It was here that Ascended Master El Morya received President John F. Kennedy after his passing in 1963. El Morya founded The Summit Lighthouse in 1958 in Washington, D.C., for the purpose of publishing the teachings of the ascended masters given to the Messengers Mark and Elizabeth Prophet, a continuation of his efforts in so many incarnations to establish the concept of God-government on earth.

Through the Messengers Mark and Elizabeth Prophet, the Darjeeling Council has sponsored manifold endeavors: the establishing of the order of the Keepers of the Flame Fraternity by Saint Germain in 1961 to set forth graded instruction in cosmic law; the founding of Montessori International by Mother Mary, Jesus, and Kuthumi, based on the principles of Dr. Maria Montessori and including the teachings of the ascended masters; the founding of Summit University; and the setting of the seal of God upon Church Universal and Triumphant, the mystery school of all of the masters of the Great White Brotherhood, and the community of souls ascended and unascended on the path of initiation, East and West, in Christ and Buddha.

You have a unique spiritual destiny. One of the keys to fulfilling that destiny is understanding your divine nature and your relationship to God.

To help you understand this relationship, the ascended masters have designed the Chart of Your Divine Self, which they also refer to as the Tree of Life. The Chart is a portrait of you and the God within you, a diagram of yourself—past, present and future.

The I AM Presence and Causal Body

The Chart of Your Divine Self has three figures, corresponding to the Three Persons of the Trinity and the Divine Mother. The upper figure corresponds to the Father (who is one with the Mother) and represents your I AM Presence. The I AM Presence is the Presence of God individualized for each of us. It is your personalized I AM THAT I AM, the name of God revealed to Moses at Mount Sinai.

Your I AM Presence is surrounded by seven concentric spheres of rainbow light that make up your causal body. The spheres of your causal body are the storehouse of everything that is real and permanent about you. They contain the records of the virtuous acts you have performed to the glory of God and the blessing of man through your many incarnations on earth.

No two causal bodies are exactly alike because their shimmering spheres reflect the unique spiritual attainment of the soul. The particular attributes you have developed in your previous lives determine the gifts and talents you will be born with in your succeeding lives. These talents are sealed in your causal body and made available to you through your Higher Self.

The Holy Christ Self

Your Higher Self, or Holy Christ Self, is depicted as the middle figure in the Chart of Your Divine Self. Your Holy Christ Self is your inner teacher, guardian and dearest friend. He is also the voice of conscience that speaks within your heart and soul. He divides the way between good and evil within you, teaching you right from wrong.

Shown just above the head of the Holy Christ Self is the dove of the Holy Spirit descending in the benediction of the Father-Mother God.

The shaft of white light descending from the I AM Presence through the Holy Christ Self to the lower figure in the Chart is the crystal cord. In Ecclesiastes, it is referred to as the silver cord (Eccles. 12:6). Through this "umbilical cord" flows a cascading stream of God's light, life and consciousness. This stream of life empowers you to think, feel, reason, experience life and grow spiritually.

Your Divine Spark and Four Lower Bodies

The energy of your crystal cord nourishes and sustains the flame of God that is ensconced in the secret chamber of your heart. This flame is called the threefold flame or divine spark. It is literally a spark of sacred fire from God's own heart.

The threefold flame has three "plumes." These plumes embody the three primary attributes of God and correspond to the Trinity. The white-fire core from which the threefold flame springs represents the Mother.

As you visualize the threefold flame within you, see the blue plume on your left. It embodies God's power and corresponds to the Father. The yellow plume, in the center, embodies God's wisdom and corresponds to the Son. The pink

plume, on your right, embodies God's love and corresponds to
the Holy Spirit. By accessing the power, wisdom and love anchored in your threefold flame, you can fulfill your reason for
being.

The lower figure in the Chart represents your soul. Your
soul is sheathed in four different "bodies," called the four lower
bodies: (1) the etheric body, (2) the mental body, (3) the desire
body and (4) the physical body. These are the vehicles your
soul uses in her journey on earth.

Your etheric body, also called the memory body, houses
the blueprint of your identity. It also contains the memory of
all that has ever transpired in your soul and all impulses you
have ever sent out through your soul since you were created.
Your mental body is the vessel of your cognitive faculties. When
it is purified it can become the vessel of the Mind of God.

The desire body, also called the emotional body, houses
your higher and lower desires and records your emotions. Your
physical body is the miracle of flesh and blood that enables
your soul to progress in the material universe.

The lower figure in the chart corresponds to the Holy
Spirit, for your soul and four lower bodies are intended to be
the temple of the Holy Spirit. The lower figure is enveloped in
the violet flame—the transmutative, spiritual fire of the Holy
Spirit. You can invoke the violet flame daily to purify your four
lower bodies and consume negative thoughts, negative feelings
and negative karma.

Surrounding the violet flame is the tube of light, which
descends from your I AM Presence in answer to your call. It is
a cylinder of white light that sustains a forcefield of protection
around you twenty-four hours a day as long as you maintain
your harmony.

The Divine Mother focuses her energy within us through
the sacred fire of God that rises as a fountain of light through
our chakras. *Chakras* is a Sanskrit term for the spiritual centers

in the etheric body. Each chakra regulates the flow of energy to a different part of the body. The seven major chakras are positioned along the spinal column from the base of the spine to the crown.

The Destiny of the Soul

The soul is the living potential of God. The purpose of the soul's evolution on earth is to perfect herself under the tutelage of her Holy Christ Self and to return to God through union with her I AM Presence in the ritual of the ascension. The soul may go through numerous incarnations before she is perfected and is thereby worthy to reunite with God.

What happens to the soul between incarnations? When the soul concludes a lifetime on earth, the I AM Presence withdraws the crystal cord. The threefold flame returns to the heart of the Holy Christ Self, and the soul gravitates to the highest level of consciousness to which she has attained in all of her incarnations.

If the soul merits it, between embodiments she is schooled in the retreats, or spiritual homes, of the ascended masters in the heaven-world. There she studies with angels and masters of wisdom who have gained mastery in their fields of specialization.

The ascension is the culmination of lifetimes of the soul's service to life. In order for the soul to attain this ultimate union with God she must become one with her Holy Christ Self, she must balance (pay the debt for) at least 51 percent of her karma, and she must fulfill her mission on earth according to her divine plan. When your soul ascends back to God you will become an ascended master, free from the round of karma and rebirth, and you will receive the crown of everlasting life.

NOTES

For the definition of many of the philosophical and esoteric terms used in *The Chela and the Path,* see the comprehensive glossary, "The Alchemy of the Word: Stones for the Wise Masterbuilders," in *Saint Germain On Alchemy* published by Summit University Press.

Chapter 1

1. Prov. 16:25.
2. John 10:10.
3. Rev. 3:21.
4. Eph. 4:22–24; Col. 3:9, 10.

Chapter 2

1. From the New Year's Eve dictation given by Gautama Buddha. Dictations are the messages of the ascended masters, archangels and other advanced spiritual beings delivered through the agency of the Holy Spirit by a messenger of the Great White Brotherhood.
2. Matt. 10:39; Luke 17:33.

Chapter 3

1. Exod. 3:14.
2. Ps. 8:1, 3–6.
3. I Cor. 13:12.
4. Matt. 24:40.

Chapter 4

1. John 8:58.
2. Gal. 6:7.

Chapter 5

1. Thomas Moore, "Believe Me, If All Those Endearing Young Charms," st. 2, lines 3–4.

Chapter 6

1. The letters used to form the words "I AM race" are taken from "A-m-e-r-i-c-a."
2. Saint Germain was embodied as Joseph, the protector of Mary and Jesus, and as the prophet Samuel, affectionately called Uncle Sam as he embodies the spirit of freedom to the American people.
3. I Cor. 6:20.
4. Matt. 5:18.
5. Acts 2:3.
6. For information on audiocassettes and CDs of violet-flame mantras, decrees, affirmations and songs, call or write The Summit Lighthouse for a free catalog.
7. *Saint Germain On Alchemy* (Corwin Springs, Mont.: Summit University Press, 1985), p. 99.

Chapter 7

1. Rev. 3:11.
2. Matt. 16:16; John 11:27.
3. I Cor. 11:24.
4. John 1:9.
5. John 3:16.
6. Acts 17:28.
7. For further instruction see Mark L. Prophet and Elizabeth Clare Prophet, *The Science of the Spoken Word,* paperback, and *The Science of the Spoken Word: Why and How to Decree Effectively,* 4-audiocassette album A7736, published by Summit University Press.
8. Matt. 7:12.
9. Matt. 22:12.
10. The calls to the chohans are made in anticipation of the ray of the day which is released to the planet from the heart of God through the spiritual sun of this solar system at midnight (your time). The rays of the days are as follows: Sunday, second ray, yellow; Monday, third ray, pink; Tuesday, first ray, blue; Wednesday, fifth ray, green; Thursday, sixth ray, purple and gold; Friday, fourth ray, white; and Saturday, seventh ray, violet. Thus when you make the call before retiring Sunday night, it is to be taken to the retreat of Paul the Venetian, Chohan of the Third Ray that is focused in the planet and her evolutions beginning midnight Sunday (12:00 a.m. Monday). Chelas are asked to retire by 11:00 p.m. so that they may be in the retreats by midnight to begin the cycle of the new day with the chohan of the ray of the day.
11. I Cor. 11:24.

Chapter 8

1. The Master is speaking of souls whose evolution is on the etheric plane. Some of these have ascended, others remain with their home star, and still others volunteered long ago to serve with the evolutions of earth. There are Mercurians who have fallen from the way of the Christ; some of these have taken physical embodiment on earth. Other Mercurians have achieved great attainment through the path of the Christ; these have won their ascension. The God Mercury and El Morya are examples of the Mercurian overcomers who may be called upon to lend their momentum of victory to earth's evolutions.
2. John 14:4–6.
3. When the Christed One realizes that his true self is the fullness of the I AM Presence, he declares, "Lo, I AM *that* I AM!" In other words he is saying, "*God in me is* the I AM." Thus whenever the chela, centered in his God-realized Self, affirms "I AM," whatever follows becomes a statement of the law of his being. I AM is therefore not only the

name of God, but it is an abbre-
viated way of declaring, "God in
me is" or, "God in me is the action of. . ."

4. Eph. 4:22–24; Col. 3:9, 10.

5. Henry Wadsworth Long-
fellow, "The Builders," st. 5.

6. John 19:23.

7. Matt. 11:28, 30.

8. *Prayers, Meditations and
Dynamic Decrees for the Coming
Revolution in Higher Consciousness,* sections I and II, published
by Summit University Press.

9. Ps. 23:3.

Chapter 9

1. Ezek. 1:4.

2. Rom. 8:6.

3. Gen. 1:26, 27.

4. Henry Wadsworth Long-
fellow, *The Song of Hiawatha,*
part 1.

5. Gen. 4:9.

6. Matt. 25:40.

7. John 16:33.

Chapter 10

1. A blue ball—the size used
in the game of jacks.

2. John 8:12.

3. Matt. 18:19, 20.

4. Ps. 104:4.

5. See Mother Mary's Scriptural Rosaries for the New Age—
one for each morning of the
week and one for Sunday evening—available on 8 audiocassettes and in *My Soul Doth Mag-
nify the Lord! Mother Mary's New
Age Teachings and Rosary with a
Challenge to Christendom,* by
Mark L. Prophet and Elizabeth
Clare Prophet. See also *A Child's
Rosary to Mother Mary* and *The
Fourteenth Rosary: The Mystery of
Surrender,* audiocassette albums.
"Watch With Me," Jesus' Vigil of
the Hours is a devotional service
to Jesus and the ascended hosts
with prayers, songs and decrees;
on 90-min. audiocassette with ac-
companying booklet. To order,
call or write The Summit Lighthouse.

6. John 1:14.

Chapter 11

1. John 5:39.

2. I Cor. 3:19.

3. Rev. 21:2.

4. Rev. 12:10, 11.

5. John 1:14.

6. John 1:5.

7. Rev. 12:7–9.

8. Rev. 1:1.

9. Rev. 12:4.

10. Rom. 8:17.

11. John 1:9.

12. Rev. 12:12.

13. Rev. 12:17.

14. Luke 17:21.

Chapter 12

1. Rev. 19:11.

Chapter 13

1. Michael delivers the
sphere of the first ray of power
on Tuesday; Jophiel the sphere

of the second ray of wisdom on Sunday; Chamuel the sphere of the third ray of love on Monday; Gabriel the sphere of the fourth ray of purity on Friday; Raphael the sphere of the fifth ray of truth on Wednesday; Uriel the sphere of the sixth ray of peace on Thursday; and Zadkiel the sphere of the seventh ray of freedom on Saturday.

2. Heb. 13:2.
3. Luke 1:38.
4. Exod. 3:14.
5. René Descartes, *Le Discours de la Méthode*, 4.
6. Hab. 2:14.
7. Ps. 101:1, 2.
8. Rev. 1:8.
9. Matt. 2:13.
10. Matt. 2:15.
11. Luke 2:52.
12. Mark 1:11.
13. Matt. 4:3; I Thess. 3:5.
14. Num. 17:8–10; Heb. 9:4.
15. Rev. 21:16.
16. Ps. 119:17, 18, 47, 48.
17. Matt. 5:3–10.
18. Ps. 110:4; Heb. 5:6, 10; 6:20; 7:17, 21.

Chapter 14

1. Sanskrit for Great Lord. Title borne by the ascended master holding the office in hierarchy of representative of the Holy Spirit.
2. Heb. 12:1.
3. Heb. 12:2.
4. Rom. 8:17.
5. Heb. 10:9.

6. Dan. 7:9.
7. Saint Germain to "Friends of Freedom," 7 March 1961.
8. John 10:9; Rev. 3:8.
9. Acts 1:9.
10. I Pet. 2:5.
11. John 8:32.
12. John 14:2.
13. Ps. 37:7.

Chapter 15

1. I Thess. 4:17.
2. Matt. 24:21, 22.
3. Mark 1:17.
4. Matt. 7:6.
5. I Cor. 13:9, 10.
6. Matt. 13:46.

Chapter 16

1. Rev. 4:4.
2. I Cor. 12:10.
3. Titus 1:10.
4. Isa. 8:19.
5. Exod. 7:8–12.
6. Ps. 103:15, 16.
7. Matt. 11:10.
8. Matt. 24:30.
9. I John 4:1.
10. John 16:23, 24.
11. Matt. 7:20.
12. Matt. 21:19.
13. Luke 11:52.
14. James 3:11.
15. Luke 17:21.
16. Rev. 19:10.
17. Exod. 20:3.
18. Matt. 22:37.
19. Mal. 3:1.
20. Rev. 12:3.
21. Isa. 55:11.
22. I Pet. 5:2–4.

ELIZABETH CLARE PROPHET is a pioneer of modern spirituality. Together with her husband Mark L. Prophet, she has published such classics of spiritual literature as *The Lost Years of Jesus, The Lost Teachings of Jesus, The Human Aura, Saint Germain On Alchemy* and *Reincarnation: The Missing Link in Christianity.*

Since the 1960s, Mrs. Prophet has been lecturing throughout the United States and the world on spiritual topics, including angels, the aura, soul mates, prophecy, spiritual psychology, reincarnation and the mystical paths of the world's religions. Her lectures are broadcast on more than 200 cable TV stations throughout the United States.

She has been featured on NBC's "Ancient Prophecies" and has talked about her work on "Donahue," "Larry King Live," "Nightline," "Sonya Live" and "CNN & Company."

Mrs. Prophet lives in Montana at the Royal Teton Ranch, home of a spiritual community where she conducts conferences and workshops.